WILD LIFE PUBLI

THE
FIERY FURNACE

A MEMOIR BY
NOW BORN
FOREWORD BY KOJO AMEEN

Publisher's Information

Wild Life Publishing Presents

The Fiery Furnace
ISBN-10: 0-692-63708-7
ISBN-13: 978-0-692-63708-1

Library of Congress Catalog Card Number:
in publication data
Wild Life Publishing
P. O. Box 78964
Atlanta, GA. 30357
WILDLIFE.PUBLISHING@YAHOO.COM

Editorial Assistants: Nailah Kennedy and Trina Lucky
Cover Design/Graphics by Drea Delgado
for KTL Graphic Designs

Paperback Design by eBook Bakery.com
Manufactured in the United States of America
The Fiery Furnace © Copyright 2016 by Now Born

All Wild Life Publishing titles, imprints and distributed lines are available at special quantity discounts for bulk purchases for sales promotion, premiums, fund raising, educational or institutional use. Special book excerpts or customized printing can also be created to fit specific needs. For details, write to Wild Life Publishing: Attention Senior Publisher P.O. Box 78964, Atlanta, GA. 30357 or visit our website at www.wlpublishing.com

First Trade Paperback Edition Printing
10 9 8 7 6 5 4 3 2

ACKNOWLEDGMENTS

This book is indubitably the most important book that I've written thus far and I wanted to make sure that the first people who I acknowledged were the most special to me. People who, in some way, helped me to evolve into the man that I am today. Chiefly, there's my mother. Thank you for always believing in me and for never abandoning me, even when I most deserved it. Thanks to my biological sisters for holding me down through all of the years that I was incarcerated. I don't know what I ever did to deserve such grace and loyalty, but you have my gratitude.

To my educator and mentor, God Amar Allah, thank you for endowing me with your supreme understanding on so many things. Even though you returned to the essence some years ago, you are still living vicariously through me. Also to Travis "Fresco" Kirkland and Lamont "Rampage" Clark. You were the two brothers that I never had and you both died too young. I will never forget you, no matter how successful I become.

I would be remiss if I didn't mention some of the brothers who I served time with in prison. Good brothers like Divine Intelligence, Born Wise, I Self, Jemo Johnson, Shateek, King David, Shaborn, Foundation, Shakur, C-Wise and Leon Gregg. Next, I want to say peace to my friends and family members in society who remained a form of contact and support for me while I was in prison. I know that its difficult to remain loyal to a person who is incarcerated - as the system, by design, severs most bonds between inmates and their loved ones. So many people couldn't endure that test of time, but you did. So...peace to Shalonda Holmes, Victorious Allah, Al Green, Teman Myers, Joy Lowery, Tony Gusto, Infinite, De'borah Bryant, Demetris Pringle, Demetrius Thomas, Marcus Kirkland, Justice Born, Melissa Tweed, Dino Davis, Marquita Hall, Ileia Belton, Ty

Equality, King Justice, Blu Butterfly, Brooklyn Lou, Justice Love, Lerell and Ieshia Morning, Cristana Smith and Supastar Ace. Finally, I want to thank you (the reader) for your support.

CONTENTS

DEDICATION

Throughout my years of incarceration, I've made friends with some good brothers from all walks of life. Some of them had twenty, thirty and fifty year sentences. I would like for all of those brothers to know that I recognize their struggle and that I respect their fortitude and endurance. However, I've decided not to include any of those names in this dedication. This book is dedicated to all of my comrades who are serving life sentences and better. Those individuals are Vincent Boseman, Kojo Ameen, Timothy "Supreme" Washington, Steven McClain, Ty Nitty, Scientist, Freddie "Panama" Butler, Charles Tyson, Day Day, ATL, Dro, William Gregg III., Lil' Rah Rah, and TJ. I want all of you brothers to remain strong and to never give up on your fight for freedom. Peace!

Your brother and companion in tribulation,

Now Born

Foreword

Hotep! Ma'at! I am a 71 years-young black Afrikan man. My attribute is Kojo Soweto Ameen, and I'm currently serving a life sentence in the devil's penal colony. I received that sentence many years ago because I dared to stand and defend a black woman's honor, and perhaps her life. I like to call this place the Department of Death. They have countless ways to exterminate us like animals. The number one way, in my opinion, is with this garbage that they call food. I've been eating this garbage for approximately 35 years now, and counting. After 35 years of this madness, its a wonder that I am still sane. At this time, I want to comment on the author. I met Now Born Allah some years ago, here in one of Babylon's penal colonies. What I like most about him is his spirit. The young God shines every time that I see him. I cannot see the pressure upon the young God but I can feel it. The same pressure is upon all original people in these days and times.

This book is full of good food for our minds and spirits. Now Born, thank you for the knowledge and truth within this book. The topics in this book can be sensitive to some of you readers. Please harden your hearts to the truth and deal with the reality of this powerful message. This young writer is audacious, his writings are provocative, and I love this book. I know that the Fiery Furnace will be an experience that we will all enjoy because it is a very clear depiction of this hell on earth that is far too familiar to so many of us. This book is informative and bold, and readers will recommend it to their friends, sure enough. All brothers and sisters on the inside of the penal system must read The Fiery Furnace. Know thy self. One heart, one love.

-Kojo Soweto Ameen

PROEM

In the many years that I've served in the so-called Department of Corrections, I have grown to understand the system for what it truly is and not what it appears to be. I know and understand that the media has the power to shape public opinion. We've all seen television shows like Cops, America's Most Wanted, Bait Car, and even the local news where brothers and sisters are constantly being funneled into the jails and prisons of America. I like to call those shows "programs" because they are intended to program the masses to perceive the United States justice system in a particular way. Some of us have become so brainwashed that we are entertained by these programs and even find ourselves rooting for the police. Every one of us has someone who we love that is entangled in the system; whether it is a brother, a father, a son, an uncle, a nephew, a cousin, a friend, or ourselves. (Females are not excluded)

Many of us forget about our loved ones once they enter the penal system and remain there for extended periods of time. Some of us are so conditioned that we honestly believe that our loved ones belong in prison. One reason for that is because of the influential power of the media. That, conjoined with the miseducation of blacks and the subconscious fear that most of us have for the law enforcement and what it represents. I do concur that certain people like rapists, pedophiles, serial killers and people with those types of mental disorders are unfit to be in society. However, prisons all over the country are over-crowded with so-called criminals who were convicted for poverty crimes. Poverty crimes are crimes that are most often committed by people in penury. They include but are not limited to drug offenses, robbery and burglary. The judges are giving out more time for poverty crimes than for murder, rape and etc. I know of several cases where brothers received life sentences simply for burglarizing homes.

I can remember one instance when I was working as a dishwasher in the cafeteria at one of the prisons that I was housed in. I was working alongside a caucasian man who was almost twice my age. I was washing the dishes and he was rinsing them. A dialogue sparked between us and I asked him what he was incarcerated for. He said that he had murdered his father-in-law. I asked him if he had a life sentence and he answered, emphatically, "No, the judge gave me 15 years". I couldn't believe my ears because I was serving a 17 year sentence for armed robbery. In my case, no one had even been physically injured. This man had shot and killed his father-in-law in cold blood and received a lesser sentence than mine. That's when I realized the racial discrimination and the disproportionate sentencing that occurs in the judicial system.

Many people perceive the Department of Corrections as a place where the criminally insane go to be reformed and made fit for society. Most of them only perceive it that way until they actually experience being incarcerated for themselves. They then realize that prison has very little to do with reform. That is totally up to the individual. Most of the prisons that I've been to offer very few programs other than religious programs. The drug and alcohol abuse programs are only made available to short-time offenders who have less than one year remaining on their sentences. One particular program that I remember is an annual Christian-based program called Kairos. Kairos allows about fifty inmates to attend a four day-long worship service in the prison's chapel. The sponsors serve the inmates delectable foods from various restaurants and treat them really kind, catering to them for all four days. They constantly sing somber gospel hymns, make prayer and share testimonies. They practically hypnotize the inmates with the food and the music.

By day four, you will see these stone cold killers crying and turning their lives over to Jesus Christ, all because they were overwhelmed by the experience. On that day, all of those inmates are asked to take a group photo. The photographer, who is one of the sponsors, says "everybody smile" just before he snaps the photo. Of course, everyone complies. They are happy because their bellies are full and they'd been catered to for four days straight. The Kairos sponsors constantly remind them that they love them and that they understand them even though no one else seems to. Most of the inmates haven't heard kind words like those in years. The group photo is posted up on the wall, in the hallways of the prison's chapel. Visitors tour the prison and see the pictures with the inmates smiling from ear to ear. Automatically, they conclude, "Wow, this place isn't so terrible after all". The Kairos program is only a ruse that is being used to cloak the harsh conditions of the prison and its financial scheme.

It's almost cliché to say that prison is a modern-day form of slavery. Sadly, the majority of the people who haven't been there don't truly appreciate what that means. I can candidly say that black people have counted for 90% of the prison population at every prison that I've been in. The so-called justice system is actually unjust. In most cases that I've seen, a black man had committed a poverty crime, for whatever reason, and had gotten arrested. He couldn't afford to pay for adequate legal representation so the judge appointed him a Public Defender. ...ple who have dealt with them before refer to them as ... and I've also heard people call them Public ...blic Defenders do is work in collusion ...nd the prosecutors to get their ...eir clients to believe that they ...g their charges. They sell them ...favorable plea bargain. When they enter their guilty pleas, they basically sign themselves into slavery. They normally don't realize, immediately, how complicated they make things for themselves by admitting their guilt. They soon realize after they begin fighting for redress from the courts.

The reason that I used the term "slavery" is because thats exactly what prison is. This country is generating more money off of it's prisoners than it was when chattel slavery was legal and blacks were cropping tobacco, cotton and sugarcane in the south. In the state that I was incarcerated in, the federal government funded the state with $30,000 per inmate each year. Even in cases when the inmates had sentences that were shorter than one year. Those funds were supposed to be used to supply food, clothing and shelter to the inmates. Most of the foods that are served in the prisons are grown on farms at various low-custody prisons throughout the state. The inmates who labor in those fields work without compensation.

Those farms also raise cows and chickens which they use to supply the statewide prisons with meats, eggs and milk. As for the clothing, the inmates manufacture the uniforms as well. The state's only expenses are the antiquated machinery and the low-quality fabrics that are used to make the uniforms. Those inmates also labor without pay. They have these sweatshops all over the state known as Prison Industries, where thousands of inmates labor for free, manufacturing uniforms and coats for the inmates all over the state. They even make shorts that are sold to the inmates, and the inmate Prison Industry workers don't receive any percentage of the proceeds. Weekly, they work for forty hours just like most of the working class in society

The prison system is a multi-billion dollar industry to the multiple ways that it siphons money from the ir and their loved ones. Each prison has a collect-callin⸵ for inmates to use. It's more expensive than the col! services that avail people in society. These collecr are a commodity because it's a basic need for the inmates to communicate with their loved ones. The collect-calling plan is pre-paid and it generates interest. The food and hygiene items that are sold in the prison's canteen are mostly generic brands that are almost expired. Those items are obtainable at a lower rate when purchased just before their expiration dates. The state also pays a discounted rate for those items because they buy them in bulk. Exclusive of that, they inflate the prices and profit in three different ways.

Quarterly each year, the inmates who have their canteen privileges are allowed to order what they call Winter, Spring, Summer and Fall Packages. They are allowed to order up to $200.00 worth of food, hygiene supplies and undergarments at inflated prices. During those times of the year, the state generates millions of dollars from those orders. Those food items are also purchased shortly before their expiration dates at discounted bulk order prices. The inmates don't receive their packages until approximately two months after they pay for them. Almost bi-monthly, each prison has what they call a Food Project. Typically, a local restaurant will be holding a special sale and the prison director will make an arrangement with that restaurant. The restaurant agrees to sell him X amount of orders at a discounted rate. In those instances, the funds are collected from the inmates almost two months in advance as well. The prison director also inflates the prices on those orders, turning yet another profit.

I can recall numerous occasions when the prison had held food projects in the visiting room while inmates were on visitation with their families and friends. Several high-ranked officers like sergeants, lieutenants and captains had pooled their funds together and bought foods to cook and sell to the visitors. Normally, they sold hot dogs, french fries, fish sandwiches and baked goods. They would cook the foods themselves and overcharge the visitors for them. The visitors knew that was probably the best meal that the inmate would've received in a while because the institutional foods are barely esculent. Needless to say, the officers always sold out. I've seen cases where the officers have held car washes in the parking lot on visitation day, offering to detail the visitors' vehicles for money. The system is so greedy that they even go as far as to recycle the soda cans that the inmates throw away. They purport that the proceeds are used to repair things within the prison.

Inmates are charged $5.00 each time that they report to Medical to be treated for an ailment. Most times, the nurses simply tell them to get some rest and they furnish them with a handful of generic ibuprofen pills. The prisons sell small television sets for about $200.00. Those same tv sets only cost $50.00 in local department stores. They also sell am/fm walkman radios for $50.00. Those radios can be purchased in stores for $10.00. These are just a few examples of how the state capitalizes off of the inmates that are being warehoused in it's prison facilities.

Another aspect of this governmental scheme that I want to address is the deliberate destruction of the family unit. Most of the prisons are located in small rural towns, secluded in remote locations. Families often have to drive for hours just to see their loved ones who are incarcerated. In many cases, the female visitors are denied entry due to claims of them being inappropriately clad. People get denied their visits for the simplest reasons, even after they have driven for hours. That discourages the visitors from returning very often. Its also compromising for the visitors when they have to undergo a search each time that they enter the prison. The inmate disciplinary system is very harsh in terms of punishment. For most offenses, inmates lose their visitation privileges for lengthy periods of time.

The men who do have their privileges aren't allowed to be affectionate with their women on visits. What usually occurs is that the women feel compelled to move on with their lives because the men are unavailable to them in necessary ways. The costly collect-calling rates cause complications because some women can't afford to accept their calls on a consistent basis. In some prisons, the men aren't even allowed to pick up their children on visits. Its also difficult to get children approved to visit inmates. Most prisons don't offer paying jobs to the inmates, disabling them from legally providing for their families from prison. Another disturbing fact about the prison system is that the inmates are not allowed to attend the funerals of their loved ones. It doesn't matter if they are the funerals of their parents, their wives, or their children. The only way that they can see the funeral service is if a family member records it on video and sends it to the prison. The prison's chaplain will inspect it and then he will allow the inmate to watch the video in the prison's chapel.

For this proem, I mainly intended to highlight some things that most of our people fail to realize about the system that we call our justice system. We need not to look down upon our loved ones simply because they are immured. There are some great minds in prison. If you have a loved one who is lost in the system, you should find them and reach out to them. You never know what that person is dealing with on a day-to-day basis.

1

One Summer Morning

"But if you do not worship, you shall be cast immediately into the midst of a burning fiery furnace. And who is the god who will deliver you from my hands?"

- Daniel 3:15

It was the morning of June 26th, 2007. I was asleep in my bedroom at my parents' house until my mother entered the room and woke me up around 6:45. I didn't even get three hours of sleep that night. I had been up all night worrying about how the next day in court was going to unfold. Up until then, I had been out on bond for over a year and a half. I had been refusing to plead guilty so that I could give myself a reprieve against going to prison. By that day,

I had bought all of the time that I could buy. My plea bargain had expired and a jury had already been selected for my trial. Allowing that plea offer to expire is one of my biggest regrets, and you will understand why by the end of this chapter. When my mother woke me up that morning, my first thoughts were to pack some clothes and leave town.

The only thing that prevented me from doing that was the fact that my mother had used the deed to her house for collateral when she paid the bail bondsman to bond me out of the county jail. Had she not done that, I would either be on the run, dead, or serving the maximum sentence that my charges carried (30 years) because I would've been tried in my absence and eventually captured. Since she did use her deed as collateral, I had to man up and surrender myself to the courts. I would've been a true scumbag if I would've let my mother lose her home and live on the streets. I love her too much to even entertain the idea of doing something like that. She knew that, and thats why she felt comfortable with using the deed to her house for collateral. When my mother left out of my room that morning, I picked up the phone and called my girlfriend (at the time). Her name was Angie. I was calling to tell her to get dressed because my mother and I would've been coming over to pick her up around 8:30.

I wanted her to be there by my side at my arraignment. When I told her, she said, "My mom is trippin' and she doesn't want me to leave the house". She was twenty years-old at the time but her parents treated her like she was a young teenager. I was twenty six. I think that her parents had the wrong perception of me and what type of person I really was at heart. I guess that one could say that I gave off a thug image, and I really didn't have much going for myself. I had actually met Angie after I got released from the county jail on bond, which

I'll admit was a bad time to jump into a relationship. I was going through so much at the time that I felt like I needed a significant other in my life. So, I went for it and I don't regret it at all because her company gave me the solace that I needed at the time. Her parents were focused on the fact that I was unemployed. A part of the reason for that was because I had been reporting to General Sessions Court five days a week, ever since I had met Angie.

I never revealed my court situation to her parents until the week of my trial, but I explained it to Angie, when we started getting seriously involved. After court each day, I would hustle in the streets for a couple of hours, then take a taxi cab to her parents' house and spend the evening with her. I guess that it didn't assuage the situation any when I always came to her parents' house inebriated on weed, with a mouthful of gold teeth and gold jewelry on. In the beginning, I even brought drugs and guns into their home. That was the lifestyle that I was engaged in prior to meeting Angie. She inspired me to slow down and put all of the nonsense behind me. The only vice that I held on to was my excessive weed habit. I had stopped hustling, robbing and the whole bit; but I would smoke weed ad nauseam. I can recall how all of my friends started telling me, "Born, that girl's got you trippin'. Now is the time that you should be robbing and hustling more than ever before".

Their logic was that I should've done something illegal to conjure up enough cash to pay off the bail bondsman and recover the deed to my parents' home. Then I could go on the run and be a fugitive like most of them were. I wasn't interested. As far as I was concerned, I was already in over my head. Like the old adage goes, "If you find that you've dug yourself into a hole, stop digging". All I wanted to do was smoke my weed and spend time with Angie. My right-hand man had just gotten murdered that year and, deep down, it was a tumultuous time for me. Another thing that Angie's parents didn't realize was that she loved the way that I treated her. Like all couples, we had our quarrels but never anything physical. That morning when she told me that her mother was trippin', that just added insult to injury. I was thinking, "I'm about to have the judge throw the book at me today and my blackwoman won't even be by my side".

She said that her mother's second reason was because Angie had been attending court with me every day of that week, and each day her mother was under the conception that I was going to get sentenced. After a few days of still seeing my face, she concluded that her daughter and I had been lying to her. And, furthermore, we probably hadn't been going to court at all. She just didn't understand the court procedure. You normally don't know your trial date until that date arrives, especially when you don't have a paid attorney. All I knew was that my time was near. I knew with certitude that this particular day was the day of my arraignment because my trial had actually been slated to begin on the previous day. I failed to appear and was fortunate not to have a bench warrant served on me. Instead, I had stayed out all day and most of the night with Angie and my friends; smoking weed and trying to build up the nerve to face the judge.

The only thing that I could think to do was ask my mother to call Angie's mother and corroborate my story. As planned, it worked and her mother permitted her to go to court with me that one final time. Thats when I started getting myself together. I took a look around my bedroom, thinking about how I wouldn't be seeing that bedroom again for more than ten years. Ten years was my original plea offer which had expired. To make matters even worse, I overheard my parents starting to argue in their bedroom. I couldn't believe that my father was raising hell about my mother refusing to give him cash to get high with. "Not at a time like this", I thought. He had no intentions of appearing in court with me that day. He was too busy chasing his next high. I stayed out of their argument until I overheard him threaten her, "Just wait until you come home from taking him to court today...". When I was growing up, my father was abusive towards my mother so that statement could've only meant one of two things.

Either he was planning to do her some type of physical harm when I went off to prison, or he was going to take some money from her that evening. When I overheard his subtle threat, I walked into their bedroom. My mother was in their personal bathroom getting dressed while they continued to level insults at each other. My father was sitting on their bed. I was so distraught that I just took a deep breath in attempt to calm my nerves. Then I took a seat at the foot of their bed. I looked at my father and the first words that I could muster were, "Dad... don't kill my mom when I go to prison". My words must've pierced his heart because he calmed down and replied, "Son, I ain't gonna do nothing". A few seconds later, they started up again but it was more calm. I walked back into my bedroom and rolled a blunt out of a dime bag of weed that I had from the previous night. Then I walked outside and smoked half of the blunt in my parents' backyard. My puppy named Cash followed me and kept me company while I smoked.

I found myself talking to him about my problems while he just stared up at me like I was losing my mind. As much as I wanted to smoke the other half of my blunt, I threw it in the dewed grass because it was getting late and I didn't want to be late for court. Well, let me rephrase that... I didn't want to hear my mother go on a tirade. I couldn't have cared less about going to court. When I returned inside, I took a quick shower and got dressed. I still had more weed leftover and it was wrapped up in some tissue. I walked back into my parents' bedroom and gave the weed to my father. He received it and told me, "Thanks son". Then he began telling me about how bad he felt about me going to prison and gave me a few words of encouragement. His words went in one ear and out of the other. I was still feeling disgruntled about him choosing not to go to court with us.

About 30 minutes later, my mother and I were both dressed so we prepared to leave. I walked in and out of every room to get one final look at my parents' beautiful home, realizing how much I was going to miss that place. Once outside, we got into my mother's all-black Chrysler 300. As she drove off, Cash was chasing the car as he usually did. I watched him and realized that I was going to miss him too. He was my first puppy and I had grown somewhat attached to him. I stared back at my parents' house until it was completely out of my view. Our first stop was at Angie's parents' house. My mother remained in her car while I walked to the door to get Angie, and to give her family my last goodbyes.

When her mother invited me inside, Angie was still in the bathroom getting dressed. The only people in sight were her mother, her grandmother, her older sister, and her sister's daughter who was still an arm baby at the time. They all knew what was going on so I began by telling them how much I enjoyed being like a part of their family for the past year or so. I thanked her mother for letting me come over everyday and I apologized for any trouble that I might've caused. As I was speaking, all eyes were on me, my voice began to crack and I shed a tear. It was a painful moment for me because I had grown attached to that family. Their house had became like my home away from home over that past year.

Her mother took my hand and we all bowed our heads because she wanted to say a prayer. She basically prayed for the best outcome in my hearing that morning. Afterwards, I hugged everyone with my eyes still fraught with tears. Angie and I walked outside and joined my mother in her car. My mother drove in the front seat, alone, while I rode in the backseat with my arm around Angie. My mother asked me if there was any particular cd that I wanted to listen to. Thats when I inserted a cd and played the song "For A Reason" by Zhane. I'm not sure of why I chose that song because that has to be the saddest song in the world. I guess that I wanted to cry. Angie and I were both silent and teary-eyed. My thoughts were scattered all over the place. Plus, I was inebriated so I was definitely in deep rumination.

The next stop was at Burger King. I don't eat meat so I ordered a cheese croissant, some hash browns, an orange juice and some cini-minis. Angie did eat meat so she probably ordered a chicken biscuit combo or something. She had stopped eating pork for me earlier in our relationship. We arrived at the court house punctually, just as everyone else was filtering in. I could feel the butterflies in the pit of my stomach. My aunt Betty Ann met us there and we all entered the edifice together. The first person that I spotted approaching us was my Public Defender. Ever since the first day that we met, her energy never agreed with mine. That morning, she came to me talking about how I could've had a bench warrant served on me for not showing up in court on the previous day. Then she practically threatened me, "Today is the day". By then, my mind was made up that I was about to plead guilty and go to prison. Within the next twenty minutes, I was standing before the judge and entering my guilty plea.

I said that I was pleading guilty on my own volition and that no one had coerced me. My aunt Betty Ann was standing on my far-left, my mother was at my immediate left, and Angie was on my right, holding my hand. The judge did his normal routine, then he sentenced me to 17 years with no remorse. He even had the audacity to say, "Good luck to you" afterwards. My ten year plea offer had just expired on June 19th and there I was, seven days later, being sentenced to seven additional years. I was then placed into handcuffs. My family was escorted out of the courtroom and into the hallway. A few moments later, I was escorted into that very same hallway so that I could board the elevator and descend down to the basement where the holding cell was located at. Just before boarding the elevator, I kissed my mother and my aunt on their cheeks. Then, I kissed Angie on her lips. Thats when two officers and I took the elevator down to the basement where I was placed into a small holding cell by myself. I didn't shed one tear in that cell. I just remained silent. The reality was still sinking in. I remained in that cell for less than one hour, then I was transported to the county jail. That was the beginning of a journey that I will never be able to forget.

2

PREMONITION

About three weeks after I was sentenced to 17 years, I was assigned to a 3-man cell at the Reception and Evaluation Center. I was there waiting to be transferred to my designated facility. The bed was three bunks-high and I slept at the very top. As a matter of fact, throughout my entire bid, I've always had the top bunk. Most inmates prefer the bottom bunk but I never understood that. I guess thats because I'm fastidious. I don't like for people to sit on my bed, and people normally sit on the bottom bunk when they visit you in your cell. Plus, when you're on the bottom bunk, you have to worry about your bunkee dropping things on your bed like clipped toenails, exfoliated bodily hair and etc.

In this particular cell, one of my cellmates was a white guy and the other one was black. I was standoffish towards them because I didn't know either one of them from Adam. Plus, I had just gotten sentenced to 17 years, so I had too much impinging on me to be socializing. I don't remember much about either one of those guys, besides the fact that I thought that they were both clowns. I think that the white guy was a methamphetamine addict because of how decayed his teeth were. He was younger than I was. The black guy was short in stature and he was always on the floor, doing push-ups. I felt like he was weird ever since this one day when a guy from another cell yelled out to him and told him to imitate Donald Duck's voice. I was expecting for him to retort back with a slick remark. Instead, he said a few lines in the Donald Duck voice for real. Whats crazy is that he sounded just like him, like he'd been rehearsing for years.

A few guys in the other cells were laughing but I just ignored him and kept reading like I didn't hear him. I didn't even crack a smile. I know that made him feel stupid because he never did it again. That first time was all that I needed to hear to realize that I didn't have any business talking to that guy. The white guy didn't get any conversation from me either. Needless to say, I did a lot of sleeping during the four weeks that I was there.

During the third week, I had a recurring dream that came to me three times. It was an awkward dream and I have eidetic memories of it. On the first night that I had this dream, I dreamt that I was perambulating through a suburban neighborhood that was unfamiliar to me. I walked past this one particular house and noticed that there was a young black girl playing on the front porch by herself. She ranged between the ages of 12 and 14 years old. As I walked past that house, a black man with dreadlocks approached the porch. I didn't pay any attention to what he did after that. I just continued walking down the street. That very same dream returned to me a day or two later. This time, I watched the man to see what he was about to do. He started out by playing with the little girl but she appeared to be uncomfortable around him. Seconds later, he grabbed the little girl and she yelled.

At that instant, I woke up and my heart was quickening like I had just had a nightmare. The dream had intrigued me so much that I closed my eyes and tried to return to it. Unfortunately, I couldn't go back to sleep. In the penitentiary, dreams are like movies for some people. Its not out of the ordinary for an inmate to tell you about a dream that they had on the previous night, explaining every intricate detail. Well, this dream had my attention and I was eager to learn what this dream-movie was going to be about. A few days later, the dream finally returned to me. It played out the exact same way that it did both previous times. Only this time, the man grabbed the young girl like he was trying to kidnap her. Then he ran towards the backyard as she kicked and screamed for him to release her. I rushed to her aide because I recognized that something was definitely wrong. Before I could reach the backyard, where he had taken the girl, I was awakened because an officer opened my cell door for some reason.

I never had that dream again after that day, but my intuition kept telling me that the dream signified something. My first thoughts were that some adolescent girl had been killed or raped by a man who once slept in the very same bed that I was lying in. And, his mind energy was somehow still lingering in that cell. A few years later, at an entirely different facility, I was assigned to a cell with a black guy who was a little younger than I was. It didn't take long for me to realize that he was a compulsive liar and that he had an imagination that was gargantuan. The average person would've deemed him as being crazy but

I saw him as somewhat of a virtuoso in con artistry. Some of his stories actually sounded plausible until I really observed his ways and actions and got to know him. For months, he had me under the impression that he was incarcerated for drug offenses. Then, he'd supposedly killed an inmate at another facility by using his martial arts skills.

There was an old man in our dorm who he alleged had testified against him in his murder trial and gotten him sentenced to 150 years. He said that this old man was at the previous institution with him and that he had witnessed the fight. I'll admit, he had me convinced for a second. I was starting to feel disgusted with the old man because snitches repulse me. After a while, I started realizing the inconsistencies in all of my cellmate's stories. I have elephant memory but he wasn't all that retentive. One day I looked him up online with my cellphone and learned that he only had 45 years. Inmates started volunteering information to me about how spurious he was and how he maligned me behind my back. Everything became clear one day when one of those guys took me to the old man who had allegedly snitched.

I didn't ask the man any questions. The guy that I was standing with did all of the talking. He asked the man if my cellmate had caught a body at the previous prison where they were incarcerated at together. The man looked at me and laughed, as if to say, "Wow, he fooled you too?". He went on to explain that my cellmate was actually in prison for beating his 14 year-old female cousin to death because they were occasionally having sex and she wanted to stop and confess their wrongs to other family members. The old man explained that he had learned that information a few years earlier when my cellmate had asked him to read over his trial transcript and help him to write up a petition to the courts for his appeal.

I assessed the situation and concluded that he was trying to turn me against the old man, as a ruse to prevent me from someday speaking to him and possibly learning about his actual charges. I started reflecting back on some of the stories that my cellmate used to tell me because there was now something eerily familiar about them. Especially the ones where he would boast about how long his dreadlocks used to be. It dawned on me then that the dreams that I had at the Reception and Evaluation Center were actually premonitions. I strongly believe that the young girl from my dream was the girl from his case.

3

The Invisible Wedge

I used to be good friends with two guys who I met at one of the prisons that I was housed in. One guy was from Atlanta, Georgia and the other one was from Washington, D.C. In prison, many times inmates are called by the names of the cities that they are from. I called these two friends of mine ATL and D.C. They were cellmates and they lived downstairs from me, about three doors down. D.C. was a muslim and ATL was trying to do the Christian thing. He wasn't your quintessential Christian though. This guy was a certified killer when he was out in society. He had life plus thirty years, plus he had pending warrants for another murder. A lot of people thought that he was eccentric and I'll admit, he was a little off the rocker. After getting to know him, I understood his story and I felt like I could relate to him in some ways. Most of the riff raff that he would speak was only because of the stress that he was under. If I had life plus pending murder charges, I'd probably lose my faculties too.

So that was my circle at the time: D.C., ATL, myself and my partner named Missouri. A muslim, a christian, a member of the Nation of Gods and Earths, and I don't know what ideologies Missouri subscribed to. I knew that religion had always been a delicate topic, and that was a boundary that we never crossed with one another. I didn't spend much time outside of my cell but, whenever I did, one of those three guys would come and build with me. The term "build" simply means to have a constructive dialogue with someone. Normally, I would be standing next to my cell with a pen and a writing pad in my hand. My pen and pad served as my "Do Not Disturb" sign. People in prison will sometimes just approach you and try to stimulate a dialogue with you about any random thing. Typically, something trivial. That always seemed weird to me because I've never been the gregarious type. When people noticed me, seemingly immersed in my writing, they knew that I didn't care to be bothered so they moved along.

Over time, I started noticing an invisible wedge between ATL and D.C. I never thought that it was anything major. I think that its perfectly normal to have fall-outs with a person when you both live in an 8X10' cell together. Especially during lockdown situations when you're locked in the cell with that person 24/7, sometimes for weeks and even months on end. I've had arguments with most of my cellmates, and I've had fist fights with two of them. Sporadically, D.C. would come to me and complain that ATL was living like a savage in their cell. Most muslims that I know are tidy and organized, as I am. So, I understood his position on this. I always tried to convince him to circumvent ATL. The main reason for that was because he didn't know ATL like I did. If he would've rubbed him the wrong way, it would've been ugly. Judging from some of his stories, taking a man's life was like lights on/lights off with ATL.

Ever so often, ATL would come to me complaining but he wasn't as petulant as D.C. was. His approach was a bit different. It was more like, "Born, your man be acting like a bitch sometimes. I be wanting to beat his ass in that cell but I'm trying to do this Christian thing". He didn't feel the least bit threatened by D.C. Their little back and forth back biting went on for about two weeks. For that entire time, I always tried to mediate the situation. I even suggested that if they couldn't learn to ignore their differences, then maybe they could've spoken to the dorm lieutenant and requested a cell change. I said that either one of them could've moved into my cell and that I would've gotten my cellmate to move downstairs. Why they never did it... I don't know.

Eventually, the inevitable happened. It was approximately 5:30 one morning when I was awakened by the sound of some ruckus downstairs. I automatically concluded that there was a fight going on in some other cell. I could hear the sounds of sneakers squeaking on the concrete floor and loud bangs every time that someone would hit the lockers in the cell. Everyone was normally asleep at that time of morning, so the dorm was completely silent. By that point, I had witnessed so many prison brawls that they didn't even interest me anymore. A fight could've broken out right in front of me and, if one of my cohorts wasn't involved, I'd likely just turn and walk away without looking back. When I concluded that the ruckus downstairs was merely two cellmates fighting, I immediately rolled back over in my bed and went back to sleep.

At 7:00, the officer would've been coming around to let everyone out of their cells who wanted to go to breakfast. I had opted to miss breakfast that morning so, when the officer opened my door, I told him that I wasn't going. Then, he locked my door and continued making his round. I returned to sleep. Less than thirty minutes later, Missouri knocked on my door. I turned towards the door with my usual early morning scowl on my face. When I noticed that it was Missouri who had knocked, I simply yelled out, "Whats up?". Then he beckoned me to the door. Whatever it was that he wanted to tell me, he didn't want to say it loud enough for anyone else to hear it. He wanted to whisper it to me through the crack of my door. I knew that it had to be urgent. Even Missouri knew not to disturb me that early in the morning because of how crossly I could be.

I climbed down from my bed, slipped into my shower shoes and slowly walked to the door. I placed my ear near the crack of my door and Missouri whispered, "You need to come out here. ATL and D.C. were fighting this morning and ATL said that D.C. is messed up bad". The officer only made rounds once every hour so I had to wait another thirty minutes before he would open my door again. I told Missouri that I needed to freshen up. Then I washed my face, brushed my teeth and got dressed. When the officer finally let me out, I walked downstairs. Thats when I spotted ATL standing in front of the Phone Room. He looked vigilant with both hands in his pants, obviously clutching a knife. I know that he was worried about the other muslims retaliating on him for what he had done to D.C. As I approached ATL, I looked around to see if D.C. was anywhere in sight. He was nowhere to be found. I saw a few muslims sparsely scattered but none of them were grouped up. They obviously had no knowledge of what had transpired.

I gave ATL a fist bump and asked him, "Whats good?". Immediately, he began to explain, "I had to bust your man up this morning". As he spoke, I sized him up from head to toe. Thats when I noticed that a few droplets of blood had stained his pants. I asked, "So, where is he at now?". His reply was, "He's in the room but he won't be coming out". Considering ATL's violent personality, my next question was, "Did you kill him?". He calmly answered, "No, but he's messed up. He probably won't be coming out of the room for the next few days". Then I lowered my head and reminded him, "Bro, I told you to move out of that room". He started to explain that he was feeling remorseful about what he had done but my mind was telling me to go and check on D.C. Thats when I told ATL that I would be right back, and I walked over to his cell.

The first thing that I noticed was the gory trail that ATL had made with his boots when he exited the room. I'm surprised that the officer didn't notice it when he had let ATL out of his cell and locked the door behind him. When I approached the window on their door, I noticed that D.C. had all of the back windows covered. The entire cell was obscure except for the small amount of light that shone in from the outside of the door, where I was standing. That light enabled me to see a puddle of blood that was in the center of the floor. There were also a few circles of blood on various sections of the wall. It literally appeared like someone had dipped a basketball into a bucket of blood, then bounced it against the walls a few times. After hearing ATL recapitulate what had happened, I learned that those circles had came from the few times that ATL had banged D.C.'s head against the walls. The walls were painted white and made of concrete.

I spotted D.C. lying in his bed, on the bottom bunk. The sheets were white so it was easy to notice that they were also covered in blood. He was lying motionless. I worried that he was dead so I tapped on the window and called out his name. He didn't budge until I called him a second time. I told him to come to the door. When he came to the door, I could see that his t-shirt was all bloody. I knew that he was embarrassed because he hid his face while I spoke to him. The only thing that I could see was his left ear, on to the back of his head. Even his left ear had a bad scar on it. I asked if he was alright. He bumped the window with his fist and gave me a thumbs-up, meaning yes. When I asked him was it over, he turned his thumb downward. ATL had already pummeled him and I knew that he would've killed him the next go 'round. I didn't want to crush D.C.'s male ego so all that I said was, "Just be careful". He turned his thumb back up, letting me know that he appreciated my concern.

When I walked back over to where ATL was standing, he was accompanied by Missouri. I posted up on the wall with them. We were all keeping our eyes on ATL's cell, to see if any of the muslims were going to approach the door. We knew that after they would've found out about the fight, it would've been on. No one ever approached his door. Eventually, the dorm officer opened the wing door and released the breakfast crowd. Seeing D.C. like that had ruined my appetite so I didn't go. ATL moved out with the crowd, still clutching the knife in his pants. Missouri decided not to go to breakfast either. We were the only two inmates left in the pod. The officer had returned to his desk in the center of the pod.

After a few minutes, Missouri and I heard a knock coming from D.C.'s door. He must've thought that everyone had left the building. He was trying to capture the officer's attention. I assume that he was too embarrassed to let everyone see him all disfigured. The officer opened his cell and immediately noticed the blood and the bruises. Thats when I was able to get a closer look at him. Both of his eyes were black, I believe that his nose was broken, and his lips were swollen. The sight of him churned my stomach. Since the wing door was still opened for the breakfast movement, D.C. hobbled out of the dorm. He was planning to walk to the medical building to seek medical attention.

Missouri and I approached him on his way out and I asked, "Are you good homie?". He tried to answer but, instead, he just erupted into tears. His words were opaque but it sounded like he was trying to say, "He stabbed me in my eye". Thats when I noticed that a chunk was missing out of his tongue. I later learned that ATL had been stomping D.C.'s head on the floor with his boots on. That caused D.C. to bite off a chunk of his own tongue. We all exited the building together. D.C. and Missouri made a right turn towards the medical building. I went left, headed to the cafeteria. I wanted to warn the other inmates that the dorm was probably about to get locked down when everyone returned from the mess hall. As soon as I made the announcement, most people left their trays on their tables and ran back to the dorm to stash whatever contraband items they had on them. If the First Response officers would've made it to the dorm before the inmates did, everyone would've been searched on the way back inside.

When I told ATL what the deal was, we both rushed back to the dorm together. We urged the officer to let ATL back into his cell. The officer unlocked ATL's door and he returned inside. He wanted to clean all of the blood up before the First Response team came in to conduct their investigation. He believed that his cell was going to be their first stop since that was where D.C.'s living assignment was. He asked me to stand at his door and to block anyone from looking inside while he cleaned up the blood. Standing at that door and watching him, thats when it was confirmed that ATL was a bona fide killer. He seemed calm and experienced at what he was doing. Also, focused. He was cleaning up the blood with wet newspapers, then flushing all of the evidence down his toilet. Next, he flushed D.C.'s bed sheets down the toilet. The toilets were high-pressured and really loud when they flushed.

After almost five minutes, I noticed five or six lieutenants coming through the entrance door. I looked around the inside of ATL's cell and he'd done a pretty good job of cleaning up the blood. One of the lieutenants ordered everyone, "Everybody stand by your doors! Lock down!". I made my way upstairs to stand by my cell door. About ten minutes after everyone was locked down, I noticed the lieutenants placing ATL into handcuffs and escorting him out of the dorm. He was placed in Solitary Confinement. In a way, I was satisfied that they took ATL off the yard. He was too priapic to admit himself into Protective Custody, so the muslim community probably would've killed him.

4

Nowhere to Run

A s I mentioned in the previous chapter, I'm in the Nation of Gods and Earths. Throughout all of my years served in prison, I've came across quite a few brothers who claimed to be in that same institution of learning. Most of them had obtained their knowledge in a different way than I did. I began learning the knowledge of self at Allah School in Mecca when I was fifteen years-old. Allah School in Mecca is the first school that was established for the Nation of Gods and Earths, in the year 1967. Its located in Harlem, New York. Most of the brothers who I met in prison had acquired their knowledge in prison.

The contrast that I noticed was that many of the brothers in prison had somewhat of a gang mentality. In fact, the Gods and Earths are considered as a security threat group in every prison that I've ever been to; just like the Bloods, the Crips, the Gangster Disciples and the MS-13's. The Gods and Earths that I came up around were viewed by society as civilized people, community leaders, and righteous teachers. After realizing the contrast between the brothers in the prison houses and myself, I took the initiative to correct the ones who lacked the proper understanding of the teachings. Some of them took heed and applied the knowledge. Others ignored it. I started to detect envy among some of them but I would still attend their meetings, just to keep the confusion down.

There were some Gods who I knew wanted to do me some type of physical harm. Right now, I want to share a story that involved a few of them. It all began one afternoon when they called a cipher (meeting) in the Phone Room. There were about 15 Gods present in that cipher. The purpose for us convening was for every God to become acquainted with every other God in that particular dorm. There was one particular brother in the cipher that day. Lets say that his name was Wise. I had been knowing Wise for about one year. After conversing with him a few times, I concluded that he was a bit mentally unstable. Therefore, my dealings with him were few. He did seem passionate about the teachings of the Gods and Earths, almost to the point where he could've been considered as a radical or an extremist.Another individual who was present at the cipher was somewhat of a new face. My assessment of him brought me to the conclusion that he didn't have it all either. He was a different kind of crazy. Like, legally retarted crazy. Lets say that his name was Gotti. That day in the cipher, everyone introduced themselves using their divine names. Like, my glorious name is Now Born Allah. Traditionally, in the Nation of Gods and Earths, the Gods' names are righteous attributes taken from our universal language, known as the Supreme Mathematics and the Supreme Alphabets. In Allah School, I was taught that our names should end in the word "Allah".

When it became time for this Gotti character to take the floor, he introduced himself using his street name which was remotely similar to Gotti. Right then, I knew that he was one of those bandwagon Gods who had no real understanding of what the nation was about. It really didn't matter to me. In my opinion, the same thing applied for the majority of the men who were conjugated in that room. At heart, I couldn't identify with most of them. I just attended their ciphers to prevent being accused of being arrogant, and to keep their envy down. After the meeting, everyone shook hands and some brothers exchanged hugs.

I attended the next cipher but I didn't stay very long. The cipher was called at the spur of the moment while I was in the middle of doing something important. A few hours later, a few of the Gods came to me and recapitulated what I had missed after I left. I really didn't care to be sucked into all of that melodrama. Gotti had said something in the cipher that pissed everyone off. He said that he subscribed to the ideologies of the Nation of Islam, in lieu of the Gods and Earths'. My take on the whole situation was, "So what. Thats that man's decision how he wants to live his life". I just left it at that.

About one week later, I was standing near the microwave in the center of the pod one afternoon. I was waiting on my turn to warm up my food. Thats when I noticed Wise and Gotti having an argument. It wasn't long before I saw Wise inviting Gotti into the Phone Room. Thats where inmates went to fight without the risk of being seen by the on duty dorm officer. I knew exactly what was about to happen and I had a good idea of what their dispute was about. Wise allowed Gotti to walk into the Phone Room first. He casually followed him inside as if they were only going inside to speak more privately. I knew

Wise and his volatile temper. I also knew that as soon as the Phone Room's door closed behind them, Wise was going to swing on Gotti.

I kept my eyes fixed on them and, just as I had predicted, Wise threw a punch as soon as the door shut. I couldn't see Gotti because he was standing behind the door, out of my view through the windows. I left my food unattended and ran into the Phone Room to break up the fight. A Blood member, who had been using one of the wall phones, had already begun trying to break up the fight. He was holding Gotti back and telling me to grab Wise. I pulled Wise back. His shirt was all bloody from the blood that had leaked from Gotti's mouth. Shortly afterwards, a few more of the Gods entered the Phone Room, and everyone who was extraneous to the nation got kicked out.

Wise and Gotti both stated their cases. Gotti admitted that he was a member of the N.O.I. and that Wise had transgressed against him simply because he had called himself God. Wise interjected and warned him, "Don't ever let me hear you say that again! No man in this dorm can call himself God unless he's a part of this nation!". Wise was so upset that his nostrils were flaring. In my brain, I was thinking, "Wow, this dude is a psycho for real". I then realized that Wise didn't appreciate the concept of why we teach that the black man is God. Its not because he joins a prison gang called the Gods. Its because the black man is literally the God of the universe. The lion's share of the so-called Gods at that particular facility were, in my opinion, Gods nominally but gangmembers behaviorally.

Many people find difficulty in comprehending how the black man is God, in the aspect of him being the creator of all things that exist. In order to understand this, one must first understand the mind in relation to the universe and everything therein. The mind is supreme intelligence which is living energy in constant motion. Energy has no beginning nor ending, and it cannot be created or destroyed. Therefore, the mind has always existed. Even before the sun, the planets, the physical man and all other matter that exists. When I say "mind", do not confuse that with the word "brain". Understand the mind as the creative faculties or the organizing properties of the universe. Before the first physical manifestation of the mind, which was the sun, our universe was infinite depth, breadth and height. The mind occupied that space in no definite shape or form.

All forms of matter that exist are only expressions of conscious thoughts that were formulated by the supreme mind at some point in time. And, all systems that function to maintain that matter are controlled by the supreme mind in it's varying stages of consciousness. Whatever the mind perceives will be made manifest in no limit of time. This universal law is commonly called the law of attraction. Although everything in creation is an expression of God, it is the vessel of the black man that contains the brain which enables him to express the mind on a supreme level. Thus, making him the supreme being.

The original man (black man) is the personification of the supreme mind (God), and all black men share the same mind on it's highest level. Being that we are universal people, and that the mind is energy, our negative and positive thoughts emanate signals into the universe which cause the necessary elements and resources to amalgamate and make those particular thoughts or ideas crystallize. This is how all things within the universe came to be. The same principle applies for the material things that we individually create, and the good or bad circumstances that we create for ourselves.

In almost every religion, God is characterized as having righteous attributes. Those attributes are merely a tribute to the black man because they define his intrinsic nature. When we witness the black man doing devilment, its because he's been so far estranged from the knowledge of himself that he has no idea of how to comport himself. In turn, he imitates the white race. Thats why so many of us pretend to be wild gangsters, thugs, killers, pimps and etc. If one traced those personality traits back to their owners, they would discover that they belong to the white race. They are the ones who can hate, kill, rob and steal while having zero qualms about it because its in their nature to do so. Most blacks who try to uphold these images know deep down that they aren't being authentic with themselves. If not, they may be mentally disordered. The wrong foods, drugs, alcohol and other poisonous substances also cause us to act other than our true selves.

When Wise gave Gotti his warning, I thought about the fact that the Nation of Gods and Earths are not the only people who bear in mind that the original man is God. And, furthermore, the Gods and Earths' lessons were written by the honorable Elijah Muhammed who spearheaded the Nation of Islam. The first lesson in the N.O.I.'s student enrollment asks, "Who is the original man?". Answer: "The original man is the Asiatic black man, the maker, the owner, the cream of the planet Earth, father of civilization and God of the universe".

I said all of that to say that Gotti was well within his rights to call himself God because thats what the black man is, regardless to what institution of learning brings him into that realization. One of the other Gods in the cipher also acted in a manner that I strongly disagreed with. He said that he didn't have a problem with Gotti since he didn't throw the first blow. He then added that, had that been the case, the Gods would've thrashed him where he stood. He went on to justify Wise's actions. My lessons state that we teach freedom, justice and equality. That wasn't equality or justice in that Phone Room. They basically agreed that we had the right to go around punching brothers in their mouths without a just cause, but people couldn't do it to us. Thats oppression, not freedom. That same brother asked Gotti if he was harboring any hard feelings towards Wise. He replied, "No". Wise said that he didn't have any further problems with Gotti either. They shook hands and we all evacuated the Phone Room.

A month passed and we had all practically forgotten about the above incident. Throughout that month, I noticed that Gotti was working-out a bit more than usual. Then, one evening, something unexpected happened. I went to dinner around 5:30. When I walked back into the dorm, there was no officer in sight and there was an awkward silence in the building. Normally when the dorm was silent like that, either a fight was going on, someone had just gotten stabbed or some type of trouble was looming. Immediately, I became alert and observed everyone. I was trying to figure out what was going on. Everyone was looking towards the showers so I walked in that direction. Then, a Blood member approached me and asked, "Thats one of your Gods, right?". Thats when I saw Wise standing in the shower. He was fully-dressed and allowing the water to stream down his face. He was standing in a puddle of blood.

When everyone had moved out for dinner, for some reason, Wise remained in the dorm. I guess that Gotti saw that as his perfect opportunity to get some revenge. He grabbed the barber's clippers out of the barber's chair, crept up on Wise from behind, and struck Wise in his face with the clippers. The clippers were heavy metal clippers. The blow had fractured Wise's nose and knocked out one of his front teeth. Witnesses told me that Gotti gave a menacing laugh right after he struck him. We didn't want the dorm officer to see Wise leaking blood like that because that would've caused the dorm to go on lockdown status. We escorted him to his cell before the officer returned to the pod. A few moments later, some other Gods entered

Wise's cell, raising hell. They wanted to serve justice on Gotti. I believe that it was more personal than anything but they said that the reason was because Gotti had deceived the Gods by pretending like the beef was squashed.

It wasn't long before they all unanimously agreed to amass their weapons and search for Gotti. Everyone evacuated Wise's cell except for Wise. I knew that it was about to get ugly. I went to one of my partners, who was a Blood member, and asked him to lend me his knife. He said that it was locked in his cell and that he couldn't get to it. So, there I was. A war was about to ensue and I didn't even have a knife. I had no intentions of harming Gotti. I was just taking precautions in case things got out of control and I was forced to defend myself. I noticed three of the Gods upstairs talking to Gotti. A Blood member was standing next to Gotti, and Gotti was still clutching the clippers tightly in his fist. The Blood member was from Gotti's hometown. I walked upstairs to hear what was being said. The Gods had enveloped Gotti and his partner in a corner. As I was approaching the scene, a group of Bloods were also approaching. They were telling Gotti's partner to stand down because that wasn't Blood business.

The guy refused to leave Gotti to fend for himself. When the other Bloods realized that he wasn't respecting their call, they turned and walked away, following their protocol. One of the Gods threw a punch at Gotti and thats when all hell broke loose. Gotti struck the God in his face with the clippers, then he bolted towards the stairs. During the fray, the Blood member got stabbed behind his left ear. Gotti slipped in a puddle of water by the upstairs showers and slid down the stairs as he attempted to make his getaway. As soon as he reached the floor, a different God stabbed him but it didn't retard him. The wing door was locked and the officer was off the wing, so he was forced to run around in circles. The guy who had stabbed him was still chasing him but he was too slow to keep up with him. The Gods were spread out all over the pod so Gotti didn't know where to run to. He just ran amuck, which was probably safer than standing still for even a few seconds.

Gotti ran up a different flight of stairs, leading to the second tier. Little did he realize, he was headed for a trap. There were three Gods, waiting with their knives drawn. When he realized that, it was too late. He looked back and two more Gods were closing in on him with their knives also drawn. They all moved in and commenced to stabbing Gotti. I saw him get stabbed at least eight times. Each time was in his shoulders and his upper back. Realizing that he had no other route to escape, he jumped over the rail. They continued to stab him as he climbed over. He landed on one knee when he reached the bottom tier. The floor was made of shiny concrete. There was another God practically waiting on him, and he stabbed Gotti twice before he could ascend to his feet.

Gotti was so filled with adrenaline that all of those stabbings didn't seem to faze him. He just catapulted himself up off the floor and sped towards the wing door. Then he banged on the door to get the officer's attention. He knew that no one was crazy enough to stab him in front of an officer and risk an attempted murder indictment. They carried Gotti out of the dorm and rushed him to medical. Then, the dorm went on lockdown status. Word got back to the dorm that Gotti was in the infirmary, still alive, but suffering from eighteen stab wounds. I honestly believe that he is going to seek vengeance on every God who participated in that melee, if ever given the chance to see them again.

5

TEARS OF JOY

Its not a secret anymore that some prisons are flooded with unauthorized items like cellphones, Mp3 players and things of that sort. I've owned a number of cellphones and, whenever I didn't own one, I always had access to them. I went for years without ever having to call my loved ones collect. I slipped up twice and allowed the officers to catch me with my cellphones. That caused me to lose my visitation privileges for three years, and also my collect calling privileges. That left me with no other option but to continue to use cellphones because I wasn't going to allow them to cut off all lines of communication with my loved ones for three years. Letters wouldn't have sufficed. I just knew that I had to learn to be more careful.

My mother didn't like the fact that I was still taking the risk of getting caught with another cellphone. On the same token, she was happy to be able to hear my voice everyday. Whenever I wouldn't call, she would become worried. I was in one of the state's most violent prisons which often made the news. I had a close friend named Shalonda who would always argue with me about me taking that risk. I understood her position but she obviously didn't understand mine. After a while, she started avoiding my calls altogether. I really don't believe that was her true reason for eschewing me. I think that she was simply looking for an exit ramp so that she could walk out of my life, for whatever reason.

One thing that was really convenient for me was Facebook. Most cellphones had internet access and a lot of us used social networks for various reasons. Some brothers used them to meet females who they could possibly manipulate into giving them cash. I wasn't interested in asking females for money. My mother and my sisters sent me cash whenever I needed it. If they didn't have it to spare, I would just manage without it. When I did meet females online, it wasn't for the purpose of manipulating them. It was because I wanted to converse with a female, since I was surrounded by men everyday. Before going to prison, I always kept a beautiful female by my side. Having a female friend to communicate with while in jail gave me the balance that I needed.

Facebook was convenient for me because it gave me access to a lot of people who I had lost contact with over the years, and it enabled me to meet some new people who turned out to be good friends of mine. Facebook also brought me quite a few disappointments; seeing photos of ex-girlfriends kissing on new boyfriends, pregnant or in wedding dresses. Or, seeing where my loved ones had posted status updates about how they enjoyed a family function that I was unable to attend.

Every now and then, I would share different posts about me feeling nostalgia. My mother started warning me to be careful with that because it made her paranoid. All over the news, they were talking about how the prisons were cracking down on inmates with Facebook accounts. I understood her concern, considering the fact that I didn't know some of my Facebook friends personally. Thats when I just started posting Youtube links for various songs that best described my overall mood for that particular day. Sometimes, I would just post a brainy quote or inform everyone about a project that I was working on. Some friends would comment on my posts, encouraging me to continue progressing. That often gave me the motivation that I needed to remain positive.

Another ritual that I started practicing was sharing a few inspirational words to help all of my Facebook friends get their days started on a positive track. I would normally write it out on the previous night, just before I laid my head to rest. Then, I would share it as soon as I woke up the next morning, usually around 7:30 a.m. I'll never forget the morning of January 3rd, 2012. A few days prior to that, I had posted the Youtube link for the song, "Tears of Joy" by Rick Ross featuring Cee-Lo. Above the link, I shared, "I don't know why but I was listening to this song today and I just started crying for no reason". For some odd reason, that song had me distilling tears and I wasn't even sad about anything. I called my cellmate's name and told him to look at me. I was smiling with tears pouring from my eyes like, "Roomdog, I can't believe this song has me crying G". He just laughed, shook his head and said, "Born, you're crazy nigga".

On the night of January 2nd, I had written something that I wanted to share on Facebook the next morning. My dorm was on lockdown for a stabbing that had occurred so I didn't wake up as early as I normally would've that morning. When I did wake up, it was about 9:15 a.m. Thats when I brushed my teeth and washed my face. Then I logged into Facebook so that I could share my status. Usually, I would share my status and log right back out without scrolling down my newsfeed. After a few seconds, one particular post captured my attention. It read something to the tune of, "Rest in Peace Travis Kirkland". Travis was my best friend ever since the sixth grade. The post was shared by a guy named Lenoxx, who was an old associate of ours. We called him Seven. By that point, I hadn't spoken to Seven in over five years. Neither did I know what his relationship with Travis was like at the time.

When I initially read Seven's post, I said to myself, "What the hell does he mean Rest in Peace Trav?". I interpreted it as an innuendo, or some type of threat aimed at Trav. Immediately, I logged out and dialed my partner Dino's cellphone number. Dino was also close friends with Travis. He answered his cellphone after the first ring and I greeted him, "Peace God. Whats Seven talking about, 'Rest in Peace, Trav', has he lost his mind?". Dino paused for a moment, then he told me, "Trav is gone, Born". All that I could say was, "What?....How?....". He replied, "He had an asthma attack". When his words registered into my mind, I dropped down on one knee as if I was genuflecting. Then I started boo-hoo crying like a child. My cellmate was staring at me. My neighbors could hear me loud and clear, and so could the four guys in both cells beneath us, downstairs. The entire dorm was silent because of the lockdown situation, so other people heard me crying also.

Those people probably couldn't figure out exactly which cell the sound was coming from. I wasn't concerned with any of that, and I wasn't ashamed to cry. When I rose to my feet, I looked at my reflection in the mirror above the sink. I was still crying. A guy downstairs yelled up to my cellmate, "Yo, whats up with Born?". He replied, "Chill out. He's serious. He just got some bad news". I tried to stop crying but I couldn't restrain myself. I had just been through that exact same experience one year before I went to prison. Travis and I had lost our other best friend named Rampage. When he got murdered, I cried and carried on the exact same way.

My cellmate knew that I was incensed and I could tell that he didn't know how to ask me to calm down. He was worried that the dorm officer would hear me and come upstairs to our cell. We had two cellphones in our cell and my cellmate had a knife and some weed. He walked over to the door to see if the officer was paying our cell any attention. Thats when he told me, "Born, the c.o. is on his way up here". I forced myself to stop crying on the outside. When the officer arrived at our door, he knew right away that I was the one who was crying. My eyes were bloodshot red and tears were still pouring down my face. He asked us, "Whats going on up here?". My cellmate answered him, "We're good. He just read some bad news in a letter". I nodded my agreement and told the officer that I was fine. Then, he walked away and returned to his desk.

If the officer would've been using his logic, he would've realized that we had to have a cellphone in our cell because he hadn't even issued out the mail for that day. I just climbed back into my bed and logged back into Facebook. I needed to check out Travis' page to reassure that this was really happening. I still couldn't believe it. I had just spoken to Travis a few days prior, and he didn't say anything about having complications with his asthma. When I visited his profile, I saw where numerous people had posted "Rest in Peace", and things of that nature. Thats when my eyes began to well-up and I began crying again. That time, I pulled my coat over my face to muffle my voice.

As I was crying, I posted something on Facebook. It read, "I'm sad right now. My best friend died last night and my eyes are filled with tears as I'm texting this". I just paraphrased that, but that was pretty much the size of it. To clear my mind, I went to sleep. When I woke up, I called my mother and my sister, Trina. They both had already heard the news. Trina said, "I found out last night. I was just hoping that I wasn't going to be the one to have to break the news to you". She gave me her condolences and, by that time, I had somewhat pulled myself together. Thats when I called Trav's older brother named Nkrumah. He was being strong about it, not crying at all. I just broke down again on the phone with him. He kept calling out my name but I couldn't answer. The same case scenario when I called their youngest brother named Marcus. I had initially called to pay my respects and they ended up having to placate me. I was on the line crying and Marcus was telling me, "I know Born, I know...".

I probably shouldn't have called them like that. They seemed to had been handling it fine prior to my calls. I wanted to call Travis' mother but I was reluctant to. When Travis and I were growing up, I used to do a lot of mischief and she never approved of him hanging around me. She never really got to know me and, for that reason, she saw me as bad company for Travis. Plus, the fact that I was in prison didn't ameliorate the situation any. With that in mind, I decided not to call her that day. On the next day, I found the courage to call and Travis' father answered. I felt more at ease speaking to him. I simply paid my respects and asked him to relay my condolences to his wife.

During that week, I reflected back on the day when I had listened to the song "Tears of Joy", and begun crying for no reason. Deep down, I believe that Travis' passing had something to do with that, even though he didn't pass until a couple of days later. A friend of mine calls those types of occurrences "ontological phenomenons". Some people call it synchronicity. I still had a voicemail message from Trav saved in the phone.

He had produced a beat that he wanted me to write some lyrics to. Throughout my bid, he would leave beats in my voicemail from time to time. Before I went to prison, he and I had formed a rap group called Wild Life. Thats what inspired the name for my publishing company.

For the next few days, I listened to that voicemail message incessantly. The beat was really soulful. The main reason why I kept replaying it was because Trav's voice was at the beginning of the message. He had simply said, "Here you go, Born". Then he started the music and let it play for about one minute and a half. I was in doldrums for that entire week. Frequently, I posted on Facebook about how forlorn I felt. My mother said that she would go to Trav's funeral on my behalf since I was unable to attend. Thats when I wrote an elegiac eulogy, in hopes of having it read at his funeral. I emailed it to my mother, via cellphone. Then she printed it and placed it inside of a greeting card. She gave the card to Trav's mother at his wake. Unfortunately, my mother said that my eulogy never got read at the funeral. I wasn't upset about it because I knew that his mother had a lot on her mind, and that my eulogy wasn't at the top of her priority list.

6

HARLEM

Another brother who I had built a good rapport with was this kid named Mario. I called him Harlem because thats where he was from. He was Dominican and black, although I understand that Dominicans are actually a part of the black nation. Harlem was almost ten years younger than I was and he was a member of the Black Gangster Disciples gang. I didn't gangbang but some of my associates did.

Harlem moved next door to me, about three years into my bid. There was a hole in the corner of my wall that was large enough for me to see into his cell. Furthermore, I could hear what went on inside of his cell, and he could hear what went on in mine. We could also pass things back and forth through the wall to each other. In the beginning, he used to annoy me because he was always yelling out to his partners downstairs.

Because of the hole in my wall, it practically sounded like he was yelling inside of my cell. Plus, he was always fighting inside of his cell. Not with his cellmate, but mostly with his fellow gangmembers. It might be 8:00 in the morning and I would hear an argument break out in front of my cell. I would still be trying to sleep. I would always hear him call someone out and invite him into his cell to fight. Before long, all I hear is rumbling next door and I can't get a wink of sleep. Normally, I would just get up and get my day started.

Harlem approached me one day. He told me that he liked the way that I carried myself, and how I didn't do much socializing. He said, "I need to be more like that because you just be chillin'. Niggas can't figure you out like that". I just added, "And, you avoid a lot of unnecessary problems that way too". My rule of thumb was, "No conversation, no confrontation". I took a liking to young Harlem because the way that he came to me was genuine. A lot of people liked my style but they didn't know how to come at me. They would always do sideways stuff like see me conversing with someone who they knew and try to join in on the conversation. Whenever that would happen, I would truncate the conversation and walk away.

Sometimes I would be sitting at a table in the mess hall, eating my meal alone. Then, they would try to sit down at my table. I felt like they had snake-like intentions because they wouldn't look directly at me. First, they would place their tray on the table while looking around like they were looking for someone. Then, they would take a seat, pretending like they had ended up at my table by happenstance. For the entire time, I'm watching them studiously while they are looking around for a ghost. I would pick up my tray and move to another table as soon as they sat down. People misinterpreted my behavior as being supercilious or rude, but that was my method of keeping snakes out of my cipher. I also loathed when people tried to ingratiate themselves with me when they didn't even know me. I always felt like they had an ax to grind when they did that.

Harlem was different. We started building on a daily basis. He had a relatively short sentence in comparison to mine. He was supposed to be getting released that same year but he had pending armed robbery charges to face once he maxed out that bid. Whenever we would discourse, the conversation would usually be about something constructive. I knew that he was getting released soon and I was trying to advise him to value his freedom. He would sometimes talk about going home to rob, sell drugs and go on the run but I always protested against it. I told him that there were many ways to get money legally and that he had the potential to do it. He was sharp for his age and I saw it in him. I also told him to face his armed robbery charges instead of going on the run.

After a while, I started noticing a slight shift in Harlem's personality. He started to speak more intellectually. He was still gang-affiliated, and he still had an affinity for carrying knives. I never felt like I needed to own a knife so, whenever someone would give me one, I'd just give it to Harlem so that he could sell it for food or whatever. I started viewing Harlem like my little brother. He would consult me for advice on random things. I gradually began to enlighten him about the teachings of the Gods and Earths. As his understanding grew, he told me that he was strongly considering pursuing the knowledge of self. His only hindrance was his gang affiliation. As I mentioned in the beginning of Chapter Four, the Gods and Earths were stigmatized as just another prison gang. If Harlem's gangster disciple brothers would've found out that he was studying God and Earth lessons, he would've been deemed as a traitor and dealt with accordingly.

Harlem used to imply to me that he felt like the members of his organization weren't on his level. That was the same way that

I felt about most of the Gods. One day, Harlem approached me and said that he didn't want to be BOS anymore. Thats another name that his gang used to refer to their male members. It stood for Brothers Of the Struggle. The women were called SOS. I didn't know much about their gang, but I knew that getting out of it probably wouldn't be easy. He never came to me for any advice on how to go about doing that because he probably already knew the only way out.

I conversed with Harlem more than I did with any of the Gods, and Harlem was around me more than he hung around the gangster disciples. We had each other's backs like we belonged to the same organization. This one particular evening, Harlem and I were talking while walking a lap around the pod. I noticed that the c.o. was making his hourly round, and he was near my cell, upstairs. Thats when I said to Harlem, "Hold that thought. I'll be right back". I needed to run upstairs so that I could get the officer to open my cell door. I didn't want to stay inside. I just needed to grab a snack out of my locker.

When the c.o. opened my door, he gave me a moment to use the restroom and then I grabbed a bag of potato chips out of my locker. Next, I went back downstairs to resume building with Harlem. Strangely, he had disappeared. I didn't feel the need to search for him so I just posted up on the wall in front of the Phone Room. Adjacent to the Phone Room was a room called the Day Room. The Day Room is where guys would go to play card games, smoke, and shoot dice. There was a door in the back of the Day Room that led to a room called the Laundry Room. Thats where the inmate laundry workers would go to separate the laundry after it got washed. There was a huge glass window at the anterior of the Day Room so I could see the Laundry Room from where I was standing.

I began to notice a few of Harlem's gangster disciple brothers walking out of the Laundry Room. Still, I saw no sign of Harlem. Moments later, I spotted Harlem coming out of the Laundry Room alone. I figured that they had just held a gang meeting. Harlem spotted me posted up on the wall so he walked directly over to me. As he got closer, I noticed that he had a few scars on his face, his hair was disheveled, and his uniform was wrinkled and soiled like he'd been fighting. His first words to me were, "Born, get me a knife". I asked, "What happened to you?". He said that the gangster disciples had violated him over a fallacious claim made by one of his brothers who was jealous of him. Then he added, "Them niggas just wanted to jump me".

As he spoke, I immediately began to observe my surroundings. I noticed some of his brothers staring at us, probably wondering what we were discussing. I didn't look at either one of them for more than one second, and I told Harlem to do likewise. Most people have the habit of looking at the people who they are talking about, giving themselves away. I tried to be surreptitious, pretending like we were discussing something totally unrelated to what had occurred in the Laundry Room. We spoke for a few more minutes, trying to look as inconspicuous as possible. Then, I bumped Harlem's fist and said, "I'll holla at you later". I was sure that his brothers were off in the distance reading my lips. I also knew that they were going to be watching my next few moves to see where I would go and who I would speak to. I had to keep them off balance so I casually walked up the stairs, posted up by my cell door and pretended like I was waiting to go inside. Like a charm, it worked. Before long, they all stopped watching me.

Shortly afterwards, another one of my partners approached me. It was ATL. I was leaning against the rail in front of my cell. I appeared to him like I was simply bored. In prison, I learned to master the art of speaking through clenched teeth, without moving my lips. Just like that, I asked him, "Do you have your banger on you?". Considering that someone might've been watching us, I told him, "Start laughing because we're being watched". I didn't take my eyes off of him for one second, hoping that he was smart enough to not start looking around. That would've given me away. He picked up fast and played it right. When he answered, "Yes", I told him that there was a situation going on. I didn't want anyone to see him passing me the knife so I told him to take it to Harlem for me. I told him to wait for at least ten minutes and to approach at least three different people before he approached Harlem.

Everything went smooth and I doubt that his brothers realized that I helped him to find a knife. Nothing happened for the remainder of that day. That night, while I was in my cell, I spotted Harlem sliding me a kite through the cranny in the wall. A "kite" is a note on a small sheet of paper. In the kite, he said that he'd realized that he was outnumbered and that he wasn't going to retaliate. He also said that he'd realized why they envied him. It was because he was going home soon. I replied to his kite and said, "There is a silver lining. You always wanted out of that gang. Now, you don't have to deal with any of them". He concurred, and then he told me that he would return ATL's knife to him on the next morning.

I began to teach Harlem some of the basic fundamentals that are taught in the Nation of Gods and Earths. In the next few weeks, he got into some trouble and was moved to another dorm. On the day that he got moved, he came to my cell immediately after he packed up all of his property. He told me that he only had two months remaining until his release date. Thats when I handed him my address book and told him to write his contact information in it. He wrote down his sister's name and her address in the Bronx. I wrote down my honorable name and my inmate identification number for him. I figured that he already knew my mailing address. That was the last time that I ever saw or spoke to Harlem.

Less than six months later, one day I was walking around in the pod by myself. Thats when I spotted Harlem's picture on the local news. It was the same mugshot that had been taken for his inmate i.d. I rushed over to the tv set, trying to figure out what the reporter was saying about him. I couldn't hear anything that the reporter was saying because I didn't have my Walkman on. The way that the tv's were set up, you could pick up the tv stations on your fm radio dial. I asked a few of the men who had headphones on, "What was the news reporter saying about that kid just now?". They all said that their attention was on a different television set. Automatically, I assumed that Harlem had went home, recidivated and was on his way back to prison.

Early the next morning, I saw Harlem's mugshot appear on a news brief. Thats when I found out what had happened. He had robbed some woman, shot and killed her in the process. Then, he ran into a Wal-Mart Shopping Center in attempts to elude the police. Once inside of Wal-Mart, he shot himself in the head and killed himself. That news really perturbed me but I didn't cry about it. I still have the address book with his handwriting in it, and I'm holding on to it as a memento.

7

THE IDIOT BOX

I was never the type to watch a lot of television in prison. When I was younger, I used to hear the older Gods saying things like, "It tells lies to your vision". Some brothers simply called it the "idiot box" or the "one-eyed monster". For some reason, those expressions stuck with me throughout the years. Don't mistake me, I'm not that rigid to the point where I'm just anti-television. When I was in society, I enjoyed watching music videos, the world news, gangster movies, Jeopardy, lecture dvd's and etc. Its just that, in prison, I didn't feel like I was in the position to be thinking about entertaining myself by watching tv. My main objective was to get out of prison, and watching tv could only have been a distraction. The prisons sold tv's but I never chose to purchase one. I always viewed it like this: When an inmate buys a tv, he's making himself at home and giving up on his fight for freedom. My attitude was always, "I'll watch tv when I get home. I don't plan on being here much longer".

I grew to dislike talk shows like the Maury Show, Steve Wilkos, Bill Cunningham and Jerry Springer. I don't appreciate the way that they exploit black people under the guise of them trying to resolve their troubled relationships and family matters. For ratings, shock value and humor they portray our race as being lascivious, irresponsible, loud, ignorant and dysfunctional. At the same time, they make whites out to be the civilized people. Seeing the power that these white men have over our race, especially our women, is difficult to stomach: How they can simply ring a bell and make two siblings fistfight. And, how they use polygraph tests and other disjunctive devices to destroy black families. It always flummoxed me to see how our women viewed these white talk show hosts as their ideal images of real men and trusted every word that fell from their lips. Then, went as far as to cry on their shoulders backstage, and thank them for opening their eyes.

I had a few cellmates who owned tv's and I would seldomly watch tv with them, if they insisted. I'll admit that it does get boring at times and television does help to break the monotony. In those instances, we were either watching the news or the local movie channels. Sporadically, the movie channels would show old movies that I remembered watching when I was home. Of course, they were always the censored versions but I still watched them and soaked up the ambiance. When smartphones hit the scene, we could practically watch any movie that we wanted to. We would even download bootleg movies that were still showing in movie theaters.

When I really became focused, most of my days were spent on studying law material, writing books, drawing up business blueprints, writing letters and working hard to keep all of my business intact. I learned to be efficient with my cellphones because I understood the impermanence of having them. They could've been here today, and gone tomorrow. Most of my calls were business related. I would also make sure that my mother heard from me everyday, unless the contraband search team was around and the phone was stashed away for the day. I also had female friends who I would call at my leisure.

Directly in front of the Day Room, there were four tv's for the inmates to watch, in the center of the pod. There were nine benches situated in front of them, seating about 25 inmates at a time. Throughout the weekdays, they played whatever was showing on the local tv stations: a few movies, sitcoms, the news, talk shows and etc. Those benches were always filled to capacity and brothers' eyes were always glued to the idiot box. They didn't appear to have a care in the world, and most of them had life sentences. What sort of disgusted me was how fanatical they would be about the sports on tv. They would refer to the teams by using personal pronouns like "we" and "us". So there they were, laughing and relaxing like they were at home watching television. They seemed so complacent. At the same time, I tried to humanize and put myself in their shoes. I didn't have anything resembling a life sentence so I really couldn't wrap my head around their plight.

I can only imagine the psychological effects of knowing that you will never be released from prison. Therefore, I didn't knock them. That just wasn't my modus operandi. On weekends, the prison allowed the inmates to watch three dvd's on the tv's that were located in the center of the pod. They would show one movie each day from Friday to Sunday. Each movie would repeat continuously for an entire day. They were usually outdated movies that staff members had donated from their personal collections at home. Very few of them piqued my interest. However, this one particular Friday morning, there was a movie showing that I didn't mind watching. It was the movie Ali, starring Will Smith. I actually had that movie in my dvd collection when I was home. After breakfast that morning, I grabbed my Walkman out of my cell as soon as the officer began making his first round.

The film still had about thirty minutes remaining before the ending, so I decided to listen to some music until the movie started over again. When the movie began, I took a seat on the middle bench, directly in front of the tv's. A lot of other men were watching the movie for the sex scenes and the boxing scenes. I was more interested in the scenes about Malcolm X's quarrels with Elijah Muhammed, Ali's complications with the law, and the way that his wife embraced the teachings of Islam for him.

That movie seemed a bit longer than the average movie length. Before I knew it, the officer was opening the wing door and releasing the dorm to go to lunch. It was around 11:30 a.m. By then, I was captivated by the film and it still had at least thirty minutes remaining. My muslim partner named D.C. and I were sitting next to each other and both of us had been hoping that the movie would end before the officer released the dorm to lunch. I don't think that either one of us had any food in our lockers, so we couldn't afford to miss lunch.

The officer always released the inmates in groups of 25, usually in two minute intervals. We both decided that we would wait until the officer announced, "Last call for chow". That way we could catch another five or ten minutes of the movie, then move out with the last group. D.C. and I walked to the mess hall together, building about different aspects of the movie. We also sat at the same table in the mess hall. (Note: This is the same D.C. who I mentioned in Chapter Three.)

While we were eating our lunches, we noticed that a few guys were leaving their tables and walking towards the window to see what was going on outside. That window provided a view of the entire yard, including the dorm that I was living in. I basically ignored the guys who had walked over to the window. I just assumed that one of the female counselors must've been walking by. It was typical to see about half of the inmates in the mess hall rush over to the window if someone announced that some women were passing by. I was never thirsty like that. Most of those guys had been imprisoned for so long that they had forgotten how to even hold a conversation with a woman. They had became socially incompetent. Whenever I saw a female who I was interested in, I would wait for the appropriate time to tell her. Thats how I was in society, and I didn't feel the need to deviate while in jail.

When D.C. and I finished our meals, we carried our empty trays to what the inmates called the "tray window". Then, we got in line and waited to be released back to the dorm. There was also a window on the exit door of the mess hall, which provided a view of our dorm. When I looked out of that window, I realized that the guys hadn't been looking at a female counselor walking by. There were five lieutenants standing in front of our dorm and there was one inmate lying on the ground. Then I noticed a group of inmate hospice workers rushing to the scene, carrying a gurney. When I realized that there was only one inmate involved in the incident, I concluded that there couldn't had been a fight. That was a good thing because a fight would've caused our dorm to go on lockdown status. I just assumed that the inmate had gotten into an altercation with a lieutenant and they ended up roughing him up a little bit.

The hospice workers placed the inmate on the stretcher and I noticed that his body seemed catatonic. They carried him to the medical building, running as fast as they could. I remember thinking, "That guy has a lawsuit on his hands if he survives this". When they resumed movement on the yard, they released us back to the dorm only ten inmates at a time. I knew right then that the dorm was going on lockdown status as soon as we returned. Normally, they would release us back to the dorm at least 25 inmates per group. When the group that I was in returned to the dorm, the first thing that I noticed was a round puddle of dark blood on the sidewalk. It was in the spot where the inmate had been lying before the hospice workers arrived. I remember saying, "Damn, the lieutenant must've slammed him on his head or something".

As I made my way back into the building, I noticed that there was a trail of blood droplets coming out of the dorm, leading to the puddle on the sidewalk. We all followed the trail inside of the sally port, careful not to step in it. Thats when I realized that the trail had begun in our pod. As we entered the pod, the dorm officer ordered everyone, "By your doors! Lock down!". By then, I knew that the inmate on the gurney had gotten stabbed in our pod but the remaining facts were still sketchy. I knew that it was a severe stabbing because there was copious blood on the floor and on the sidewalk. I still didn't know who the victim was, nor the culprit.

I made my way up the stairs towards my cell as I followed the bloody trail with my eyes. I was almost aghast to learn that the trail had begun directly at the bench where I had been sitting while watching the Ali movie. The dorm remained on lockdown status for approximately one month after that incident. Later on that week, I learned what had actually happened. The victim had died before the hospice workers even made it to the medical building. The man who had stabbed him didn't even live in our dorm. He had came out of place from an entirely different dorm. It turned out that the victim was in prison for raping the man's niece, and the man found out that they were in the same prison. A witness told me that the man entered the pod while the wing door was still opened for the lunch movement. He asked that witness where he could find the man (rapist) because he had no clue of what he looked like. The witness didn't know why he was looking for the man. He just pointed him out.

The man was seated in the exact same spot where I had been sitting about twenty minutes earlier, watching Ali. The victim wasn't paying any attention to his surroundings. He was fixated on the tv screen. The man from the other dorm crept up on him from behind and stabbed him in his neck. The victim didn't even see it coming, and there was no officer present. The culprit made a clean getaway, making it a cold case. The victim hobbled out of the dorm and collapsed on the sidewalk. I didn't know the victim so I wasn't affected by the situation. I was just irate about being locked down in my cell for an entire month. Looking back on that day, I'm just happy that I decided to go to lunch. That victim could've been me.

8

E OVER I

During the first year of my last bid, I encountered a lot of upsets. I was still trying to cope with the death of my friend, Rampage. Plus, I was having a hard time being away from my girl, Angie. My father got shot. My sister was in an abusive relationship. My aunt Betty Ann got diagnosed with breast cancer. And, everyday I was faced with knowing that I had pled guilty to a 17 year sentence. Things were so heavy on me that I even tried to turn to religion and play the Jesus card. I had decided to discard all of my previous studies that debunked Christianity: The true history of the Trans-Atlantic slave trade, King James, Constantine, Pope Gregory, Pope Urban II., the crusades, and so on. I was dealing with what my friend named Great Mind Allah called "E over I", which stood for "emotions over intelligence".

That phase actually began on the day when I learned that Rampage had been murdered. I began to analyze my life and everything that I was going through. Then I remembered how my mother always taught me that the Bible taught that blasphemy was deemed as the unforgivable sin. I thought about the fact that I had been in the Nation of Gods and Earths ever since I was 15 years-old, calling myself "God" for 12 years by that point. Then I started to question, "Could that be the reason for all of the quagmire in my life?". I had recently lost the woman who I was enamored with, prior to my relationship with Angie. I was going through a crisis because of that. When I would build with some of the Gods, I would make humor of that separation by calling it the "deportation of the moon". The Gods and Earths know exactly what that means. Others may not.

So, Rampage was deceased and my woman had moved on. It felt like I was going through what Elijah Muhammed called the "Chastisement of Allah". I started letting myself go. I let my bills get backed up and I ended up losing my crib. Then I had to move back into my parents' house. I had totally retrogressed. When I thought that things couldn't get any worse, I caught an armed robbery beef and I was facing up to 30 years in prison. Going through all of that, I began to deliberate what my mother had said to me concerning blasphemy. It wasn't long before I fell prey and began to seek refuge in Christianity.

I got bonded out of the county jail and I met Angie shortly afterwards. Her family was heavily involved in the church. Her father was a deacon and her mother was an usher and a choir member. I started attending church with them, occasionally. A part of me was only trying to convince her parents that I was good enough for their daughter, since her previous boyfriend was a military man. It was blatant that they preferred that she got back with him because they kept an 8X10" photograph of him on their living room wall.

I still held on to some of the practices that I had learned while in the Nation of Gods and Earths. I still refrained from eating pork and I convinced Angie to stop eating it also. She loved to kiss and I used to always say to her in the beginning, "No lips that touch swine will touch mine". I actually enjoyed the church thing. The concept of "letting go and letting God" seemed convenient. What I was dealing with felt like too much to bear so I figured, "Why not forward all of my problems to this mystery God and let him work them out?". I was so nonplussed that I started believing that this merciful God was going to soften the judge's heart on the day of my trial and set me free because of my faith in him.

What a fool I was. The judicial system has nothing to do with faith in a mystery God. Its all about money, as I explained in the proem of this book. The system is callous towards the black man, regardless to what his religion is. Their only concern is getting you convicted. Even after the judge gave me 17 years, the veil remained over my eyes. I was still looking at my situation like another test of faith from the mystery God. I went to prison and had relinquished most of my bad habits. I didn't drink, I didn't smoke, and I had stopped using profanity. I wouldn't even contact any of my female friends, other than Angie, observing the Christian laws on fidelity. I was going to the chapel every Sunday morning for the church service. Plus, I was praying every night. I also attended the Kairos program that I mentioned in the proem of this book. I still went by the name "Now Born" because thats been my name since I was a teen. My nieces and nephew all called me uncle Now Born, so I held on to that name.

It wasn't long before the test of faith started getting harder and harder. Thats when my father got shot and I was stressing about going home to hurt the guy who was abusing my sister. What really pushed me over the top was when Angie started pulling away from me. First, the amount of letters and visits from her began to dwindle. I could tell that she was becoming lonely out there. Even when I was home, and we were together, I knew that she was the type of woman who had to have a tangible relationship with her man. I knew that because, when we started dating, she was actually engaged to the military guy. At the time, he was overseas serving in the war. Still, I decided to delude myself and believe that with me things would be different.

One night, after about eight months into my bid, I decided to give Angie a call. We hadn't spoken for a week because she was out of state with her family. They had went to North Carolina to attend a funeral. During that time, my aunt Betty Ann was ailing with breast cancer. When I called Angie on this one particular night, she was attitudinal. Thats when she confessed that she was sleeping with another guy. I let her have her say and I put on this veneer like I wasn't fazed by her words. Then she repudiated me, stopped writing and visiting me altogether. That separation tore me apart because, prior to me going to prison, I had spent every single day with her for over a year.

After we broke up that night, I walked back to my cell and climbed up on my bunk. Then, I pulled my coat over my face. I dropped a tear or two underneath that coat, feeling jilted. Over the next couple of weeks, I kept calling Angie and trying to persuade her to get back with me. She wasn't interested. I couldn't believe how brazen she was about hurting me. Back then, I didn't have much access to cellphones so I would call my mother collect and she would call Angie on 3-way for me.

I'll never forget this one day when I called home to speak with Angie. My mother accepted my call but she said that she didn't really have time to call Angie for me. She was on her way out of the door, headed to the hospital to visit her sister, Betty Ann. I begged her to call Angie, insisting that I wouldn't speak for long. Eventually, she conceded and called her for me. When we got Angie on the line, she was still acting all cavalier about the break-up like I never mattered. We hung up, then I thanked my mother for calling her. That night, I found out that my aunt Betty Ann had died just minutes before my mother arrived at the hospital. I felt guilty because I knew that it was my fault that my mother didn't make it to the hospital in time to hear her last words. That was the first time in my life that I had ever heard my mother cry. I lamented that night, thinking about everything that was going awry in my life. Then I began to rethink the whole God thing out.

First, I questioned it like, "Who does this God think I am? Job?". It seemed like my problems were being exacerbated and this God wasn't solving any of them. My mind was in a blur. Eventually, my faith waned and I slowly came to remember that there was no mystery God. I disenchanted myself and realized that I had allowed my emotions to supersede my intelligence. No mystery God could get me out of prison. And, no mystery God could bring Angie back to me either. I also realized that it wasn't the ideologies of the Gods and Earths that had failed me. Instead, I had failed the ideologies of the nation. In society, I was the antithesis of what the Nation of Gods and Earths represented.

I was telling lies, robbing, getting inebriated, mistreating my black woman, and a host of other things. The Gods teach that the black man should stand upright, be all-wise, civilized and dignified. When I realized my mistakes, I turned in my Jesus card and repatriated with the Gods. I realized that my destiny was in my own hands. If anyone could set me free, it had to be me. Considering that I had pled guilty to my crime and the overwhelming inculpatory evidence that the state had against me, I quickly concluded that it would be impossible to get my conviction overturned. Although the idea was ill-advised, escaping seemed to be my only option at the time. I didn't realize that the same key that was used to lock me up, was the same key that could set me free. In other words, my only option for freedom was to learn the law and to appeal my sentence.

Pretty soon, I began to contrive an escape plan. All of my hopes were dashed and I was beginning to feel like I had nothing to lose. I was so determined to escape that I ripped up all of my court transcripts and flushed them down the toilet. The legal route had been officially ruled out. Deep down, I was scared to death about escaping but I was still determined to leave whenever the opportunity presented itself. I began to canvass the other inmates around me, seeking out accomplices. I believed that having someone complicit with me would've obligated me to go, no matter how afraid I was. Soon, I met this mexican guy. I called him Vato Loco. He spoke broken english but I overheard him saying to someone that he wanted to escape. As desperate as I was, those words sounded crystal clear to me. I started building with him.

Vato Loco didn't have the same zeal that I had and, deep down, I knew that he wasn't built for what I had in mind. It didn't matter because I had enough enthusiasm for the both of us. A person had to really be deathstruck to try to escape from that prison because it was virtually impossible. If anything would've went awry, we both could've been shot and killed. I was desperate though, still dealing with E over I. I devised a half-ass plan that would've definitely gotten us killed. We just psyched ourselves out to believe that it would've worked. We had taken a few bed sheets and torn them into strips. Then we braided the strips together and made a ladder. We had found a 2X4" board that was about 2.5 feet long. That was used for the top of the ladder. There's really no need for me to explain the entire plan because it was far from being fool-proof. Its actually mortifying to talk about it. Lets just say that the ladder would've been used to scale the fence, even though the fence was covered with razorwire.

Time progressed and it was the week of our planned escape. Neither one of us wanted to risk being caught with the materials for the ladder in our cells, so we allocated them in a stash spot that we had found. Two nights before our planned escape date, I brought the materials into my cell. I cut a long slit in the side of my mattress and stashed the materials there. We lived in the so-called honor dorm which rarely got searched. I had to work in the cafeteria at ten o'clock on the next morning.

At work, the 12:30 count came around and all of the cafeteria workers were told to go into the dining area to be counted. I looked out of the window and spotted three contraband officers walking towards my dorm, pulling a large yellow cart. They walked into my dorm. I tried my best not to panic. There were at least 400 other inmates who lived in that dorm so the odds seemed to be in my favor. Within the next ten minutes, I saw one of the female contraband officers exit the dorm. She was coming towards the cafeteria. Thats when I panicked. She came in and immediately began talking to the kitchen supervisor. It was obvious that she was looking for someone.

My friend named Fred was standing with me so I told him to go and eavesdrop on them. A few moments later, he returned and said that the woman was looking for me. When she found me, she escorted me back to my dorm. We arrived there and my cellmate was sitting on the floor outside of our cell. I knew that they had discovered everything because the 2X4" board was leaning against the wall next to my cell. Two officers were still inside, ransacking our cell. I owned up to the materials and the officers said that I was being charged with possession of contraband. I had unbraided the sheets so they had no idea that they were actually materials for an improvised ladder. I didn't care about the disciplinary. I was just relieved that I wasn't going to solitary confinement. As far as I was concerned, I was escaping on the next morning. I easily could've found more sheets for another ladder that night.

After they searched my cell, they exited the building. I cleaned up the mess that they had left in our cell, and headed back to the cafeteria. On my way there, I noticed that Vato Loco was on the yard. He was headed back to the dorm but I had no clue of where he was coming from. I told him that the contraband team had just left my cell and that it was a close call. Then I told him to find more bed sheets while I was at work because the escape was still slated for the next morning. I went back to work and everyone was asking me if everything was copacetic. I just replied, "Yes", and returned to my work station. I was a dishwasher and they called my area "Pots 'n Pans". After about one hour, a contraband officer came into the mess hall and took me to the Maximum Security Unit. He said that I was being placed under investigation. They also took my cellmate to the Maximum Security Unit.

I ended up staying in my Maximum Security cell for exactly six months. One day, I received a kite from one of my friends back in the so-called honor dorm. He told me that he had found out that Vato Loco was the one who had sent the contraband team to my cell. He told them that I was trying to coerce him into escaping with me. I don't know why he went out like that. He could've just told me that he wasn't interested in escaping. Thinking back on that day, I realized where he was coming from when I spotted him on the yard. He had just snitched on me. I can't really be upset about my escape plans being thwarted because Vato Loco probably saved my life.

9

LOCK UP

Inmates call the Maximum Security Unit "Lock Up". The six months that I served in Lock Up were a hell of an experience, in the literal sense of the word. I only went outside for fresh air twice during those six months, and each time was for one hour. I received showers only three times a week and sometimes less. Plus, the water was usually freezing cold. The meals were meager and there wasn't any potable water in my sink to drink. I would pour myself a cup of water and I would have to let it sit for approximately two minutes. Then, this white residue would rise to the surface. I would use my plastic spork to remove the residue from the water. Once I got most of it out, I would drink it.

My cellmate for 5 1/2 months was an older man named Panama. He was serving a life sentence and had been in prison for more than 25 years. Panama had a lot of wisdom. We never had one serious argument. I used to believe that I was a good chess player until I played against him. We played almost every-day for hours, and I might've won twice. I used to write a lot of rap lyrics in that cell and he used to like to listen to me recite them. He wasn't your typical 60 year-old. He was up on everything. Every new rap song on the radio, he knew it. Plus, he spoke with all of the latest slang.

We saw a lot of crazy things while in Lock Up. The night time was the craziest. There was this white guy down the hall from us who was in protective custody because he had been raped by his old cellmate. His old cellmate was a black guy. Ever since that happened to him, he'd been shell-shocked. Every morning around 3:00 a.m., he would yell under his door, "Black nigger, stink nigger bitch!", "Black nigger, stink nigger bitch!". He would drone on for about one hour, repeating that same phrase. Some brothers would entertain it and argue with him. Panama and I simply ignored it. We knew that he was only saying that because he was in that cell where no one could get their hands on him.

Lock-Up was filled with weirdos. This one black guy used to kick on his door for hours every night, as hard as he could. Between each kick he would yell, "I wanna go home God damn!". For hours...."I wanna go home God damn!" (Boom) "I wanna go home God damn" (Boom).... I used to find it hilarious but it eventually became annoying because it was causing me to lose sleep. There was another black man named Pollock who would attempt suicide almost every other day. He would cut himself with almost anything that he could find. He wasn't very articulate. When he spoke, he had terrible sentence structure. His famous line was, "I'm the real suicidal". They kept him confined in a Crisis Intervention cell. In those cells, they strip inmates completely naked and the only property that they're allowed to have is a sleeping bag. They're not even permitted to have a toothbrush because they could possibly make a weapon out of it and mutilate themselves. Those cells also have surveillance cameras in them, being monitored 24/7.

There were inmates in Lock Up who would defecate in their palms and throw their excrement on the walls of their cells. Some of the white guys in the regular cells like ours would try to hang themselves with their bed sheets. To agitate the officers, inmates on the top tier would do what they called "Make it rain". They would stuff their bed sheets or uniforms into the toilets, then flush them over and over again. The water would eventually overflow and flood their cells. Then it would seep under their doors and flood out the top tier. Next, the water would fall from the top tier and there would be water all over the bottom tier as well. Each time, other inmates would have to clean it up. I never understood their logic behind making it rain.

Panama and I had a terrible leak in our cell whenever there was torrential rain outside. The water would flow down the wall and onto both of our beds. I hated when it rained because we always used up all of our toilet paper, trying to sop up the water. I also used to do a lot of stressing over Angie in Lock Up. I didn't receive one letter from her for that entire six months. I would grieve over losing the woman who I was with prior to Angie just as much, if not more.

This one particular morning, it was approximately 6:30 a.m. The officers had just brought a white man to Lock Up from general population. Our cell was only three doors down from the entrance/exit door, so we heard them as soon as they brought him in. He was raising hell and the sound had woke us up. He was ranting, "You get your hands off me! If you put me in that cell, I'm gonna kill myself!". Everyone was yelling for him to shut up as he passed by their doors. In a matter of seconds, I was back in La La Land.

After about fifteen minutes, I was awakened once again by a sound that was coming from directly above my head. It sounded like someone was in the cell above us, banging something heavy on the floor. The thumps were repetitious, about one every five seconds. Our ceiling was made of pure concrete and so was the floor in the cell above us. Technically, their floor was our ceiling. Judging from the thumping sound, I could tell that the person was banging with a solid object. I got irritated so I banged on the ceiling with the side of my fist and told the person upstairs to kill the noise. The banging persisted but the thumps kept getting slower and slower. When they finally ceased completely, I struggled to resume sleeping.

An officer began doing his hourly cell check on the bottom tier. Panama had gotten up and begun washing his face. I was still lying in my bed. A few minutes later, we both heard the officer running down the stairs and screaming into his Walkie-Talkie radio, "We need medical on the southside! We need medical!". Hearing that caused me to hop down from my bed. I wondered what the emergency was. A few nurses and inmate hospice workers rushed into the building. Then they all darted up the stairs. Thats when I heard the cell door above us open up.

Panama and I were both looking through the narrow Plexiglas window on our door. We knew that the nurses had to pass by our cell because we were near the exit door. Moments later, they all came back downstairs and the hospice workers had a white man on their gurney. When they brought him closer to our cell, we saw that he was disrobed down to his boxers, and he was covered in blood from head to toe. I later found out that he was the same belligerent man who had came into the building yelling that morning. The thumping sound was actually him banging his head on the concrete, attempting suicide. While the officer was conducting his cell check, he discovered the man lying in a pool of blood that had spilled from his head. I don't know whether that individual died or not.

10

THE NUMBER OF THE BEAST

Throughout my life, I've been in prison a total of three times. The first time was when I was twenty years-old. I was sentenced to 1 to 6 years under the Youthful Offender Act, for strong armed robbery. I only served eleven months on that bid before I was reposited into society. I was then placed on parole and I violated the conditions within a year's time. I went on the run and didn't get caught for over a year and a half. When I did get caught, I was sent back to prison and I served exactly one year. I returned home with good intentions but it wasn't long before I got over my prison hangover and recidivated. When my woman decided to leave me, my life really began to spiral out of control. I ended up catching a charge for armed robbery before I even maxed out my parole.

About two years later, I was sentenced to 17 years. (12 years for armed robbery, and a consecutive 5 years for illegal possession of a loaded firearm during the commission of a violent crime)

In all of my years of being incarcerated, I've had at least 100 different cellmates. They came in all different ethnicities, sizes and personalities. The only type of cellmate that I never had was a homosexual. If I did have a cellmate who was one, he concealed it well because I never detected it. My persona made it clear to everyone that I detested homos, so fags knew to keep their distance. A homo couldn't even ask me what time it was. In the mess hall once, a homo noticed me carrying my breakfast tray over to the tray window. I still had two boiled eggs on my tray. As I walked past him, he asked, "Excuse me but are you gonna eat those eggs?". When I realized who was speaking to me, I turned around and said, "Hell no, I'm throwing them away". Then, I did just that.

Only about five percent of my cellmates were white. I practically had to teach each one of them to keep the cell cleaned to my standards. Some of them, I had to make take regular showers. I'm a virgo so I'm finicky like that. Most of them smoked cigarettes but I didn't. Whenever they smoked, I asked them to stand on the toilet and blow their smoke into the exhaust vent above the toilet. This one particular cellmate that I had was a white guy who called himself Chickenman. He was a real nutcase. He actually resembled a chicken in the face. I assume thats how he acquired the moniker when he was younger.

Somehow, Chickenman started to believe that he was half man/half chicken. Sometimes I would be inside of the cell, writing or reading. Then, out of the blue, he would make a clucking sound like a chicken. I'd just look at him, shake my head, then resume reading. I wasn't at all threatened by him.

I just tried to ignore him as much as possible. Sometimes he would be standing at the door and staring out of the window. His back would be turned towards me. I would look over at him and he would have both hands on his hips, pretending to have wings. Every few seconds, he would lift his right leg and do a little backwards kick like chickens do when they scratch the ground. I used to think that it was funny when he had first moved into my cell. After a while, it got saturated and, eventually, annoying.

I soon realized that Chickenman wasn't as crazy as he pretended to be. He played crazy to prevent guys from beating him up or extorting him. When I realized that he enjoyed making a fool of himself, I started using him for entertainment. He became my jester. When he was my cellmate, I used to smoke weed. We didn't have cigarette lighters so we had to make what we called a "wick", using the electrical outlet in our cell. We had to place two metal razor blades or pencil leads into the sockets, then make them touch each other. That would spark a flame. A wick is a piece of tissue that you use to catch the flame. Then, you light your joint or your cigarette with that. If you're not careful, you will electrocute yourself. Chickenman always walked around the cell barefoot. I didn't like playing with electricity so, whenever I wanted to smoke, I would tell Chickenman to make me a wick. I almost died laughing every time that he tried because he would electrocute himself at least 3 times before he would spark a flame.

He would flinch before the razors even connected because he knew that he was about to get electrocuted. He never realized that he was only getting shocked because he was standing barefooted on a concrete floor. I knew it all along. I tolerated Chickenman for about three weeks. That was until I went to court for three days and left him in the cell by himself. As soon as I returned and walked into the dorm, everyone began telling me how Chickenman had been wilding out in our cell while I was gone. On late nights, when the dorm became silent, he had been making loud chicken sounds under the door. A few people heard rumbling sounds coming from our cell. When they asked Chickenman what he was doing, he said that he was flying around the room. Even though none of my belongings were in the cell while he was going crazy, I decided that he had to move out. Thats when I kicked him out of the cell and a black guy named Waleed moved in. He was civilized and we got along like brothers.

Later, I ended up having another white cellmate. His name was Jett. Jett was one year younger than I was. He openly admitted to smoking crack and he was always looking for cigarettes, weed and alcohol in the dorm. In the beginning, the cell was completely silent most of the time. I wasn't the type to initiate a conversation, and he didn't know how to break the ice with me. He was one of those white guys who had been in prison for a while, and he was privy to the underworld aspect of the penitentiary. He had a few hustles. He knew how to make knives and he was adept in repairing broken electronics. He knew about most of the gangs and what they were about. Also, the religious groups. Another thing that he was somewhat familiar with was the Nation of Gods and Earths.

He knew that I was a member of the Gods and Earths. He also knew that the Gods and Earths teach that the white race is a race of devils. Thats probably why he didn't know how to come at me, believing that I was a racist. I didn't hate him for being white. I deal with reciprocity so I respect everyone who respects me. Hate is only time and energy dissipated, and it requires a lot of energy to hate someone. I simply understand people for who they are and deal with them accordingly. I don't go around calling white people devils, even though thats my overall perception of the white race. I would only tell them that they were devils if they asked me. Then I would explain how and why.

Jett lived in my cell for approximately six months. We actually became pretty cool. I would even share my food with him from time to time. I would listen to his life stories sometimes and even share a few of my own. He was a Wiccan and an anarchist so, ever so often, we would converse about governmental conspiracy theories and things like that. I was careful not to offend him by calling white people devils, although he would always see me reading books by Elijah Muhammed, who held no punches. Also, Final Call newspapers. He would see Gods come to our cell door to talk to me, using expressions like "devils" and "crackers", with no regards for his feelings. Jett never mentioned it to me but I knew that it flustered him deep down.

One particular night, I was reading an article in the Final Call newspaper. Jett asked, "Born, do you mind if I ask you a question?". When I said that I didn't mind, he said, "I want you to break down to me why you all teach that you are gods and that we are devils". I knew that an honest answer would've ruffled his feathers so I said, "I don't want to go into this with you because you might feel offended". He insisted that he only wanted to learn, and he said that he wouldn't get offended. I still said, "I'd rather not". He persisted until I finally relented and started breaking it down to him. I explained it to him in storybook form, and it went something like this:

A little over 6,000 years ago, 20 miles outside of the Holy City of Mecca, a child by the name of Yacub was born. In english, his name translates to Jacob. During Yacub's time, there were no caucasian or white people on the planet Earth yet. Everyone was black. For over 500,000 years the black man has written his history in advance, once every 25,000 years. That 25,000 year history is called a Quran or Bible. The Quran that we are currently living out is the 24th Quran that has been written since the original man (black man) began recording his history 25,000 years in advance. In this particular Quran or Bible, it was predicted by the 23 wise scientists who collated it that this child named Yacub would be born in that region and during that time period. It was also predicted that when he became a man, he would make the devil. Before his birth, black people ruled the planet Earth in harmony and lived righteously in accordance with their divine nature.

Blacks didn't deal in lies, trickery, lust, hate or envy. We were all-wise and civilized. When Yacub was a child, one day he was in his uncle's backyard rubbing two pieces of steel together. When he pulled them apart, he recognized that there was a magnetic attraction between the two objects. One piece had magnetic and one piece did not. That discovery taught Yacub the rudimentary laws of attraction, that unalike attracts and alike repels. That gave him the idea of one thing controlling another. Yacub went to his uncle and told him, "I know what you know not". Thats when his uncle, who was knowledgeable of the Quran, realized that Yacub was the child who the 23 scientists had predicted.

Yacub was born with a determined idea to make a race of people, or devils, to rule over the black nation for a period of 6,000 years. They were to rule by employing devilment, lies and trick-knowledge. In order to fulfill this prophecy, that determined idea needed to be nurtured so Yacub was sent to the best universities within the Holy City of Mecca. He became a very wise scientist. He learned that within the black man's sperm there exists two life germs. One is a black germ and the other one is a brown germ. The black germ is the dominant germ and the brown germ is the recessive (weaker) germ. Yacub realized that if he could separate the brown germ from the black germ, he could graft a weaker people with a lighter skin complexion.

He also realized that if he could successfully eliminate the black and the brown germ completely, he would have made a race of people who were 100% weak and wicked. The devil.

When Yacub decided on which method he was going to use to graft the black germ out of the black man, he began going around the city and seeking out followers. He went around teaching that he knew of a way that he and his followers could rule over their own people in that city. Then, ultimately, rule the entire world. Seventy percent of the populace were satisfied with their social status and their living conditions. Yacub was able to convince the remaining thirty percent to follow him. They had expressed that they were somewhat dissatisfied. That thirty percent of the population was approximately 60,000 people. When the king learned about this scientist named Yacub and his teachings that were permeating the holy city, he immediately had him apprehended and jailed. He then realized that arresting Yacub was futile since he still had such a huge following roaming the streets of the city. Thats when the king decided to pay Yacub a visit in jail.

The king told Yacub that he didn't care what he taught. He just couldn't continue to teach it in the holy city. He agreed to give Yacub and his followers their own island where they could teach whatever they desired to teach. He also agreed to supply them with enough food to sustain them until they were able to function as an independent nation. That particular isle is situated in the Aegean Sea and it was called Pelan. In the Bible (Revelations Chapter 1, verse 9), its called Patmos. Among Yacub's followers were doctors, ministers, nurses and cremators. They were all Yacub's assistants while manufacturing the devil.

Yacub taught them all stringent laws concerning birth control. During this epoch of history, everyone was darkly complected but some people were remotely lighter than others. The doctors' law was to examine all of the couples who desired to marry each other. He would then give them bogus blood tests. If a couple consisted of two partners who were too dark, the doctor would lie to them and say that their blood wasn't compatible. Therefore, they weren't permitted to marry. If one partner was dark and the other partner was lighter, or if both partners were lighter, they were qualified to the minister. He would marry them and permit them to procreate. During parturition, a nurse was always present. If the nurse thought that the baby's head was too dark when it came out, she would inject a needle into the brain of the baby and kill it during the delivery.

If the baby didn't die from the injection, it would either be fed to a wild beast or taken to the cremator to be burned. The nurses would lie to the mother. They would tell her that her baby was an angel baby, that it was carried off to heaven and that, whenever the mother died, he or she would have secured for her a home in heaven. If the baby was brown, it was allowed to live. The nurse would tell the mother that her baby was a holy baby, that she should educate it well, and that someday he or she would become a great man or woman. Yacub also had methods that he used to thin the blood of his followers.

After following that grafting process for 200 years, Yacub's followers had successfully removed the black germ from that island. The entire populace was of a brown skin complexion. Yacub had died at the age of 150 years-old. After he died, his followers continued to enforce his birth control laws. They were all placed under the death penalty if they failed to carry them out. Another 200 years of that exact same process and the germ had transitioned from brown to yellow (what we commonly call redbones). After another 200 years, the germ became white and weak; and it was no longer original. It was 100% weak and wicked, the exact opposite of the original man. The first whites looked like what we call "albinos". They were made with a devilish nature - an innate inclination to rebel against nature, simply because the way that they came into existence was unnatural. Their weakness was their wickedness. So, it took 600 years to graft the devil on the island of Pelan.

The devils went into the Holy City of Mecca to cause trouble amongst the righteous people, just as it was predicted of them to do. When the people of the holy city first came in contact with them, they looked askance at them. The devils spoke their language. They lied and said that they were our brothers and sisters from another land, and that their skin only looked that way because they were badly mutated. During those times, our people were naive to lies and deceit, so we believed them. We embraced them, provided them with food, clothed them and sheltered them.

They gallivanted around the city while telling lies, stealing and causing mayhem. It got so bad that the original people in Mecca began fighting and killing one another. This transpired for a period of six months before we realized that they were the root cause of all of the confusion. We rounded up all of the devils that we could find, repossessed everything from them except for their language, and relegated them out of the city. A caravan of armed soldiers with swords chased them across the hot Arabian desert and into the caves of Europe, on the hillsides of the Caucusus Mountains. Thats how they became known as "caucasians". They inhabited those caves for a period of 2,000 years. The caves were guarded day and night by Turkish soldiers carrying swords. If a devil ever stuck his head out of the caves, one of the soldiers would've decapitated him.

The caves weren't very tall on the inside so the devils had to slouch in order to travel throughout the caves. Eventually, they began to walk on all fours. Because of that, most devils today have bad posture. They even developed tails to help with their balance while walking on all fours. Some whites still have vestiges of a tailbone. The caves were extremely cold. Their bodies began to adapt to the climate over time, and they became a very hairy people in order to remain warm. Sometimes they even wore the skin of dead animals. Black people have wide nostrils because of the climate in the motherland, where we originated. Because of the heat there, our wide nostrils enabled us to breathe in enough cool air to cool our brains. In the caves, the devils' nostrils began to constrict because of the cold air to their brains; thus causing them to have pointed noses.

The devils went completely savage, lost all knowledge of themselves, and began living a beast way of life. They traveled throughout the dark caves in the nude while feeding on raw dead animals, and also committing acts of cannibalism. They practiced homosexuality and sexual immorality with animals like jackals that frequently visited the caves. They contracted many diseases while living in the caves. One of those diseases was syphilis, a venereal disease that the women contracted by allowing the jackals to lick their vaginas. Thats where cunnilingus (oral sex) originated from. This is also the period when their hairy bodies became infested with the insects known as lice.

Eventually, they were allowed to come out of the caves and dwell on the hillsides. On those hillsides, they began swinging from treetops and often continued to walk on all fours. There is no history of monkeys existing prior to this period. (Note: Its not coincidental that the monkeybars are a central figure in our public school playgrounds.) They lived this way until a prophet named Musa came to civilize them. Musa translates into english as Moses. It was predicted by the 23 scientists that Musa would pull the devils out of the caves, teach them how to live a respectable way of life, how to build homes for themselves and, most importantly, the forgotten trick-knowledge that Yacub had taught them. Musa, just like Yacub, was properly taught and groomed for his mission. Then, he went on to civilize the devils so that they could fulfill the prophecy of their 6,000 year reign.

Musa had a difficult time civilizing the devil. At first, he was afraid of them so he slept inside of a ring of fire. He killed the devils that he decided were beyond reform. The others, he slowly taught. The first devils who he civilized became known as the Orthodox Jews. Even today, they adhere to the laws of Musa (Moses). Their holy book is called the Torah, or the Pentateuch, which are the first five books of Moses. Ever since Musa civilized the devils, they have permeated the entire world; ruling and conquering every nation by lying, stealing and killing. They have had only three major civilizations. The first was Greece, the second was Rome, and the tertiary but most powerful one is the United States of America.

My cellmate, Jett, sat quietly as I explained the history of his people. I could tell that he was offended. Albeit, he was interested to hear more. He asked me if the Quran or Bible that I had mentioned was the same Bible that we have nowadays. I answered, ambivalently, "Yes, and no". I explained that the so-called Holy Bible has been mixed, diluted and tampered with. This was wrought by the caucasian man with his various translations, which were intended to suppress the truth about our history and theirs. I told Jett that I could still show him that history in the Bible if he wanted to see it. He grabbed a King James version of the Bible out of his locker and handed it to me.

I began with Revelations 13:18 where it reads, "Here is wisdom. Let him who has understanding calculate the number of the beast, for it is the number of a man: His number is 666". I told him that the white man's number is six. I refreshed him on what I had said about Yacub being 6 years-old when he had played with the two pieces of steel; how it took 600 years to make the devil, how they were made to rule for 6,000 years, how Yacub had approximately 60,000 followers, and how the devil caused chaos in Mecca for 6 months. I reminded Jett that Yacub had died at the age of 150, and that the sum of 1+5+0=6. Then, I explained that even the devils' time system is predicated upon the number six. Thats why they have sixty seconds in a minute, and sixty minutes in an hour. They teach that a day is 24 hours-long, and the sum of 2+4=6. The original man knows that an actual day is 23 hours, 56 minutes, and 46 seconds long. Thats exactly how long it takes for the Earth to make one complete revolution on it's axis.

I noticed that Jett was wearing a chronographic wrist-watch so I told him to observe the number 12. Then I asked him what number was directly across from it, and he saw that it was the number 6. I told him that if he subtracted 6 from 12, the difference would be 6. Then, I told him to go counter clockwise, doing that same operation, five more times (making a total of six times). As he did it, he thought out loud, "11-5=6, 10-4=6, 9-3=6, 8-2=6, and 7-1=6".

When he asked me to show him the history about the white man being grafted from the black man, I began with Genesis 1:26 where it reads, "Then God said, Let Us make man in Our image, according to Our likeness; let them have dominion over the fish of the sea, over the birds of the air, and over the cattle, over all the earth and over every creeping thing that creeps on the earth". I explained that this verse was speaking about the black man (God) deciding to make a devil to supplant him and rule for 6,000 years. Thats why the passage reads, "Let Us make man in our image". The word "us" is plural, and it represents the black man; not some spook in the sky. Making man in our image means giving him dominion to rule over the earth, as we always have. I pointed out the fact that the devil now has dominion over the sea (The Navy and the Marines), over the air (The Air Force), and the land (The Army).

Next, I went into the Bible's version of the history of creation, and how it teaches that God created the world in six days and rested on the seventh day. Thats when I turned to Second Peter 3:8 where it reads, "With the lord one day is a thousand years, and a thousand years one day". I explained that the six day creation only symbolized the making of the devil's world which was made to last for only 6,000 years. Then, they would be deposed. Thats when the original man would be able to rest peacefully, on the seventh day. The number 7 represents God. So, the seventh day is God's day. Thats when the black man returns to the proper knowledge of himself and assumes his rightful position as king. "Mankind" being made on the sixth day symbolizes the 600 years that it took to make the devil.

I showed Jett Yacub's grafting process in the Bible. I took him to Genesis 30:31-37. As aforementioned, Yacub translated into english is Jacob. Verses 31-37, in allegory form, explain the grafting process. Concerning the devil being chased out of Mecca, I showed him Genesis 3:24. Concerning Musa civilizing the devil, I showed him the first 5 books of Moses (Genesis, Exodus, Leviticus, Numbers and Deutoronomy). I pointed out that there was much mention about caves and mountains in those books, like Mount Sinai and Mount Hor to name a couple. I showed him, in Leviticus, where Moses was trying to civilize the Israelites. He had to teach them not to eat blood, nor savage animals. He taught them not to worship idols, plus laws concerning a skin disease called leprosy. In Leviticus Chapter 18, he taught them not to have coitus with their parents, siblings, cousins, aunts, uncles and etc. The Israelites are the children of Israel. Genesis 35:10 tells us that Jacob (Yacub) and Israel are the same person.

After presenting this biblical evidence, I told Jett that being a devil was in his nature. I explained that this was why his body was laden with tattoos of demons, devil heads, fire, skulls and things like that. Thats why he loved heavy metal music which consisted of lots of noise and yelling. "Thats because of your wild nature", I told him. That also explained why white people enjoy doing things like sky diving, bull riding, bungee jumping, speed racing, deep sea diving, and other death defying stunts. And, what are those stuntmen called? "Dare devils". Then, I went into how they were the creators of horror movies, Halloween, haunted houses, and roller coasters. I realized that I was going too far when I mentioned mud racing, mud wrestling, and how pigs also loved to play in the mud.

I could see the angst starting to ooze out of his pores by that point, so I returned his Bible to him and resumed reading my Final Call newspaper. From that moment on, I could feel the dissension growing between us. We still spoke at times but I could tell that he was feeling some type of way. One Friday afternoon, he and I got into an argument about something. He had been drinking this prison wine that they called "buck". It was during 12:30 count-time and we were locked inside of our cell. I had not seen my ex-girlfriend, Angie, in over one year. I had spoken to her on the phone earlier that week and she said that she would consider visiting me along with my mother on that particular Friday. I was anticipating her visit.

When the argument started between Jett and I, visitation would've been starting in about two hours. I began putting my hygiene items into my shower bag, preparing to take my shower. I turned my back on Jett for one second and he found the chutzpah to punch me in the back of my head. It didn't hurt, but it caused me to snap. Thats when I dropped my shower bag, turned around and started waling on him. I gave him a swift right, then a left, then another right. He didn't know that the God had hands like lightning bolts. The second right dropped him and he fell into the corner by the door. He landed on his back. I stomped him a few times, then I hopped on top of him and began feeding him blows to the face and head. He was swinging aimlessly and it was ineffective because he was all drunk and groggy. I had pinned him down. He was calling me a nigger and everything. Soon, I heard the c.o. making his way towards our cell. He was on the top tier, opening all of the doors because the count had cleared.

I stopped hitting Jett and told him to calm down so that I could let him up. I said, "If you want a round 2, we can fight again when I return from my visit". He didn't want to leave me with those bragging rights. Thats when he sunk his teeth into my left wrist. It broke my skin but it didn't hurt. I punched him with my right fist and told him to chill again, because the c.o. was getting closer to our cell. I wasn't trying to let anything prevent me from seeing my mother and Angie that day. When the c.o. unlocked our door, he didn't notice us on the floor. He continued walking and unlocking the other cells. I punched Jett one final time and got off of him. He was shaking it off while I grabbed my shower bag and exited the cell. Seconds later, here comes Jett running out of the cell in his socks, throwing up his guard. He was making a big scene, saying, "Come on nigger! Come on!". The c.o. spotted us so I gave him a look that read, "Thats all him. I'm not doing anything".

Jett rushed me, saying, "You ain't God, Born!". Then he swung at me and we locked up. He tried to wrestle with me but I just threw up both of my hands. I saw the c.o. approaching and clutching a can of pepperspray. I was trying to convince the c.o. that I wasn't trying to fight, so that he would still allow me to receive my visit. Jett wanted to throw me over the rail but I put all of my body weight down and he wasn't strong enough to lift me. The c.o. drew his pepperspray and sprayed both of us in our faces, surprisingly starting with me. The first response call was made, we were both handcuffed, then escorted out of the building. I couldn't see anything because I kept my eyes shut for the entire walk to the medical building. I did that to prevent any further burning, especially from the sunlight. In the medical building, they sprayed our eyes out with cold water.

The officers took both of us to another building where there were two empty holding cells. I was placed into one, and Jett was placed into the other one. The cells were contiguous, and I could hear Jett yelling out threats for the entire time. I just laid down on the stone slab in the holding cell with my eyes shut. I was wondering if Angie and my mother were already in the visitation room waiting for me. I already knew that, if so, my visit was going to be canceled because of the fight.

It turned out that my mother did come and try to visit me that day, but Angie didn't. Jett was sent to Lock Up for threatening the c.o. who had sprayed us with pepperspray. They allowed me to return to my dorm and I was locked in my cell for ten days, on Pre-Hearing Detention. When I went back into my cell, the officers hadn't packed up Jett's property yet. I was upset that he had caused me to miss my visit so I went into his locker and stole all of his unused bars of soap, and his stamped envelopes. Plus, he had a brand new pack of white t-shirts. I took them too, as petty as it sounds. I saw Jett a couple of years later and he actually spoke to me. I didn't even mention the fight, nor the fact that he had called me a nigger. And, he didn't bring up the fact that I had stolen his things. Until this day, I still have his bite marks on my wrist.

11

THE QUEEN OF MY HEART

One person who never turned her back on me during any of my bids was my mother. She was always there for me in every way that was possible to her. She always accepted my collect calls, she wrote me letters and sent me "Thinking of You" greeting cards. She sent me money for canteen whenever she could, and she visited me frequently. When I was growing up, I would never kiss my mother. I don't believe that any of my siblings ever kissed our mother either. That was a tradition that we just didn't practice in our family. One day, while on visit with my mother, I told her that I wanted to kiss her cheek after every visit as a token of my love and appreciation. She was surprised, and also pleased with the idea. From that point on, I kissed my mother on her cheek after every visit. She was shorter than I was so I would sometimes kiss her on her forehead. After a while, it became almost routine. Before she would leave, she would lean towards me so that I could give her my usual kiss goodbye.

My mother tried to make it her duty to visit me every weekend and, most times, she came alone. On my last bid, I only saw my father once within the first six years. My parents lived together, only 45 minutes away from the prison. I never held that against my father. I still called him from time to time and expressed that I loved him before I ended each call. The policy at the prison stated that, if I only had one visitor, we had to sit directly across the table from one another. That was usually the case with my mother and I. When I would arrive in the visitation room, she would always be sitting at the table and waiting for me with a bright smile plastered across her face. She normally would've already went to the vending machines and bought us enough snacks to last throughout the duration of the visit. That was to prevent us from having to walk back and forth to the vending machines. We just wanted to enjoy the few hours of my visit by sitting together and conversing about various things.

My mother kept me posted on what the family was up to, how my dog Cash was doing, and which of my friends she had seen or heard from lately. She would usually have a message from one of my nieces or my nephew, telling me that they missed me and couldn't wait to see me. I would tell my mother stories about some of the things that I was seeing inside of the prison. Plus, I kept her informed on the constructive things that I was doing. I went through a phase when I really started working on my righteousness. Thats when I started to confess certain things that I had done in my past, which she probably would've never found out about. They say that confession and forgiveness are good for the soul. I confessed to simple things like times when I had lied in my past, and deplorable things like when I had finagled some cash out of her when I was addicted to marijuana. She forgave me for everything and I felt disencumbered to no longer have that guilt on my conscience.

As my mother sat across from me in that visitation room, I would sometimes ask her to place her hands in mine. I would flip them over, palms up, and rub them to feel what the texture was like. Before she finally retired from her job, my mother had worked laboriously for many years at General Electric Medical system, doing manual labor. Her hands were strong. Another thing that I paid close attention to was her skin. I watched her studiously, looking for any wrinkles. I studied her hair to see if she had any new gray strands. And, I always looked into her eyes. My mother strongly resembled her older sister, who I called Aunt Belle. Aunt Belle looked much older than my mother did and I always believed that my mother would look like her when she became older. Aunt Belle had these grayish highlights around the irises of her eyes. I understood those to be indicative of her aging. Eventually, I started noticing those very same highlights in my mother's eyes and thats when I began to worry.

I had a friend in prison named Kojo. He was around 70 years-old and had been incarcerated for over thirty years when I met him. He and I became good friends. He was a Rastafarian and he had a lot of wisdom that was akin to the wisdom of the Gods and Earths'. I remember him telling me the story about how he had lost his mother during his years in prison. He said that he had watched her age from behind those walls. She had went from walking on her own to walking with a cane. Then she became too decrepit to visit him anymore. He shared his memories with me about the last time that she visited him before she passed away.

Kojo's story unsettled me because I realized that he was once who I was. He was once this young man who was around 30 years-old, fresh on a protractive bid. It also disturbed me to know that my incarceration actually contributed to my mother's stress and could've caused her to age faster than she normally would have. I really began to panic one day on visitation when my mother told me some of her plans concerning her will, and who she wanted to leave certain properties to when she died. I felt horrible because I realized that I was killing my mother by being away like that. I was her only son and I knew how much she cared and worried about me. That was obvious based on the numerous times that she had taken me back into her home when I was younger, after my father had kicked me out. And, the many times when she had bonded me out of jail. Plus, the way that she used to bend over backwards to get me the things that I wanted as a child.

Knowing that I had lots of prison time over my head, the only thing that I could do was encourage her to practice healthy dieting, to get her proper rest, to drink 8 cups of water per diem, and to strive not to let things stress her out. I would advise her not to over-exert herself because she was a very hard worker. She never smoked anything, or imbibed alcohol. She had been grappling with high blood pressure and hypertension for many years. She always blamed it on stress but I knew that her standard American diet (commonly called the Sad diet) was also a factor. Ever since I came into the Nation of Gods and Earths as a teenager, I'd been trying to encourage my mother to stop eating pork. She'd been eating pork for her entire life and had grown to be stubborn in her ways. I could never persuade her to stop. Not a visit went by without me emphasizing the fact that I wanted her to stop eating swine. In her mind, she would always look at it as "that old muslim stuff".

My mother viewed my culture like she did the muslims' because we used expressions like "Allah", "Islam", and "Mecca". She was a devout Christian and, like most Christians, she wasn't open to learn any other doctrines. I noticed that the pork issue always seemed to put a damper on our visits. Therefore, I began putting it into the letters that I would write to her instead. In those letters, I kept in mind the cognitive dissonance that she had for anything that challenged or questioned her Christian beliefs. Therefore, I kept all religious dogmas out of my letters. Since Christianity seemed to be where she drew her strength from, I actually encouraged that she attended church, prayed and fasted. My concern, by that point, wasn't her religion. It was her health. That trumped everything else. In those letters, I would only address the unhealthy medical aspects of eating pork.

I began by explaining to my mother that the pig is one of the ugliest and filthiest animals on the face of the planet Earth. We (blacks in America) were taught to eat the pig's flesh after arriving on the shores of America when we were made slaves. The slave owners would eat the choiciest parts of the pig and give the slaves the leftovers: the feet, the tails, the ears, the snouts, the entrails and etc. Until this day, uncivilized blacks will proudly boast that they eat the pig "from the rooter to the tooter". I told my mother that the wrong foods make you act other than your own self.

There's an old saying that goes, "You are what you eat". I explained to her that when she consumes the pig's flesh, she also consumes the pig's blood and it's DNA which consists of it's genes. Genes determine behavioral traits. Pigs are savages and they don't have any shame. Thats why most heavy pork eaters are shameless and they seem to not have tact. They are loud and often dysfunctional in their behavior. They are also typically obnoxious, two-faced and spiteful. Some pork eaters don't fit that paradigm, although most of them do. Pigs will eat anything that you place before them and when people eat pork, that indicates that they would likely do the same thing. That explains why most pork eaters are gluttonous. Pigs love filth, and the typical pork eater's attention is easily kept by filthy things. They are also unclean regarding their living standards.

I then went on to explain the physical hazards of eating pork. The pig's flesh consists of billions of worms of various sorts. One worm is known as the trichina worm. Trichina worms are parasitic worms, meaning that they are blood suckers. They are so tiny that they can only be seen by using a microscope. When the eater consumes the pig's flesh, they also consume these worms. The worms form in small packs called cysts. Once inside of the body, the worms become multiplicative by the millions. The first place that they begin to attack is the digestive tract (alimentary canal). This could ultimately cause the stomach virus that is called trichinosis.

The worms subsequently make their way to the spine and the spinal cord. They begin eating away at the spine, gradually causing spinal problems. Every single nerve in the human body is connected to the spinal cord. The worms then attack those nerves. The effects of that, we commonly call "bad nerves". The long term effects are what we see in our elderly family members when they can't seem to remain still. Their hands and other body parts are trembling beyond their control. Thats because they have permanent "bad nerves", literally. Literally because the worms have damaged them.

As the worms travel up the spinal cord, they begin to eat away at your brain cells. The short term effects of that are short term memory loss and other malfunctions that will show through your behavior. The long term effect is what doctors call Alzheimer's disease. The protein found in pork and other meats contains a high concentration of uric acid which cannot be broken down by the liver. In turn, that acid gets deposited into the joints and ultimately causes arthritis. Eating pork also causes high blood pressure, nausea, hypertension, rheumatisms, chest pains, heart attacks, strokes, and some forms of cancer (including breast cancer and prostate cancer). I even explained to my mother that eating swine takes away a person's beauty. All of that wasn't enough to convince her to stop eating pork. I considered the fact that she was passionate about the Bible, so I decided to illustrate my points by using Bible scriptures.

I began with Genesis 1:29 where it reads: And God said, "See, I have given you every herb that yields seed which is on the face of all the earth, and every tree whose fruit yields seed; to you it shall be for food". The only thing that she could gather from that was that I was trying to persuade her to become a vegetarian. Then I referred her to Leviticus 11:7 where the prophet Moses said, "and the swine, though he divides the hoof, having cloven hooves, yet does not chew the cud, is unclean to you. Their flesh you shall not eat, and their carcass you shall not touch. They are unclean to you". She replied with Matthew 15:11 where Jesus allegedly said, "Not what goes into the mouth defiles a man, but what comes out of the mouth, this defiles a man". I retaliated with Matthew 5:17 where Jesus also allegedly said, "Do not think that I came to destroy the Law of the Prophets. I did not come to destroy but to fulfill". If the Mosaic law forbade the consumption of swine, then Jesus came to fulfill that same law.

I showed my mother Matthew 8:30-33 where Jesus casted the demons into the swine. To elaborate even further on Jesus' misprision for the pig, I showed her Matthew 7:6 where he said, "Don't give what is holy to the dogs; nor cast your pearls before swine, lest they trample them under their feet, and turn and tear you in pieces". Next, I directed her to Proverbs 11:22 where King Solomon said, "As a ring of gold in a swine's snout, so is a lovely woman who lacks discretion". When that wasn't enough, I referred her to Isaiah 66:17-18 where it reads: "Those who sanctify themselves and purify themselves, to go to the gardens after an idol in the midst, eating swine's flesh and the abomination and the mouse, shall be consumed together", says the Lord..

My mother was confused by that verse so I explained that the pig was made by the Arab scientists during Moses' time. They grafted the pig by splicing the genes of the cat, the rat and the dog. The pig was made to dispose of the wastes and human remains surrounding the caves, so that Musa (Moses) would feel more comfortable with going to civilize the caucasians. Being a mixture of cat, rat and dog, the pig will practically eat anything that you place before him, and he won't stop until its all gone.

All of that talk about why my mother shouldn't eat pork just fell upon deaf ears. In her opinion, she didn't eat much pork anyway. But, whenever I would randomly ask her what she had eaten that day, majority of the times there was some pork involved. Even after I realized that she wasn't going to stop, I still reminded her about the harmful effects of eating pork from time to time.

My mother would always be proud whenever I would tell her about some of my future prospects and the positive things that I was doing to occupy my time. She would always tell me, "As long as you're alright, I'm alright". Even when something was troubling me, I tried my best not to speak to her about it. I found that difficult during times when I didn't have a female companion to communicate with about personal issues. Sometimes I would just call my sisters and build with them instead. I didn't want to raise my mother's blood pressure by causing her to worry about me. I understood that any additional stress at her age would've been a disservice to her.

My mother was happy about the trajectory that I was on, and thoroughly impressed when I self-published my first book from prison. It was an urban fiction novel that I entitled Moving Target. I initially released it in my baby sister's name, Lavonda Wilburn. I did that for multiple reasons. One reason was because, when we were kids, I wasn't the best big brother to her. I used to ridicule her instead of defend and protect her. I even mimicked my father by being physically abusive towards her. I never really hurt her but I would hit her in her arms and legs hard enough to make her cry.

Just before going to prison to serve my 17 year sentence, I visited Lavonda in Atlanta, Georgia for one week. She was residing there at the time. That week, we got along better than we ever did as children. We were inseparable. When I went to prison, she wrote me regularly in the beginning. In those correspondences she explained to me that she had always looked up to me. I didn't realize that when we were kids.

When it became time to publish my book, I released it in Lavonda's name to show her how much I loved her and how contrite I felt on account of how I mistreated her. I had behaved that way out of sheer nescience and I strongly regret it, even though we were only children. A lot of people used to ask me, "Why did you release your book in your sister's name? She's gonna receive all of the credit". I would simply reply, "Some people prefer to shine through other people". I wasn't concerned with the accolades that I might've received because of the book. I knew that I would shine regardless, because of my righteousness. And, regardless of whose name is on the cover of the book, its always going to be my energy that the readers feel when they read it.

12

WAR IN HEAVEN

When I got released from Lock Up, I was assigned to live in a cell with a younger brother named Ra. Ra was studying the ideologies of the Nation of the Gods and Earths. He was a neophyte, or what we called a "new born". Overall, I was happy to be in a cell with another God. He was under the tutelage of a guy whose name I'd prefer to exclude from this book. Lets just say that his name was Dumbass. There was an older God named C-Wise who had the other Gods in that dorm pretty organized when I came out of Lock Up. He was somewhat of a pundit and most people were in awe of his broad vocabulary after hearing him speak. The Gods were holding ciphers once a week, and civilization classes once a week. Before I'd went to Lock Up, C-Wise was one of my closest cohorts. He was the only person, besides Vato Loco, who I had revealed my escape plans to. Thats besides one or two others who I had indicated them to when I was seeking out an accomplice.

I attended the Gods' vapid ciphers on a consistent basis. Being in those ciphers always underwhelmed me because I was the most knowledgeable in the cipher, other than C-Wise. Most of the other Gods had recently came into the knowledge of self and they didn't seem to be very earnest about the culture outside of their meetings. Therefore, I didn't take the meetings seriously either. I only went out of respect for C-Wise, to support him. Every night, Ra and I would build on different things. I came to realize that some of the lessons that he was taught by Dumbass were inaccurate. After building with me, Ra said that he wanted me to educate him, in lieu of Dumbass. I didn't want to do it initially because I believed that I would've encountered some flak because of it. I had already began to pick up on negative vibes from some of the Gods. I would hear rumors about them accusing me of being pedantic, controversial and arrogant behind my back.

Ra continued to ask if I would teach him 120 degrees. 120 degrees is the body of lessons that we are taught to learn and memorize verbatim in the Nation of Gods and Earths. They are in the form of a catechism, and we apply those lessons to our everyday lives pursuant to the dates of the month. There are actually 122 lessons totaled, but two of the lessons repeat themselves, making it an actual total of 120. Eventually, I agreed to teach Ra. I said that I would go to Dumbass on the following morning and tell him what my plans were. He was short in stature and I recognized early-on that he had a Napoleon complex. With that under consideration, I was careful not to offend him.

I greeted him with "Peace". I didn't say anything about the lessons that he'd given Ra. I just said that I thought it would've been a nifty idea for me to teach Ra 120 degrees, since we lived in the same cell together. Dumbass' exact response was, "I don't mind at all. I've heard good things about you and I believe that he's in good hands with you". With his consent, I commenced to teaching Ra his lessons. I took him back to the fundamental basics, called the Supreme Mathematics. Ra was really inquisitive and he was learning fast. In a month, he had elevated to what we call the Lost and Found Lesson #1 (1-14).

One Saturday morning, the Gods conducted a cipher. The way that the cipher operated was like this: Each God would explain their understanding of the lesson for that particular date. When Ra took the floor, he quoted the fourth degree in the 1-14. Then he explained his understanding of that degree. Everyone seemed shocked and I noticed that Dumbass looked defeated, obviously because he wasn't as effective with his method of teaching. After the cipher, C-Wise made his closing statements as he usually did. Then he asked everyone, "Does anyone have anything that they would like to say before we close out?".

Dumbass cleared his throat, raised his hand and said, "I just have one thing that I want to say. I want to know why my student is quoting lessons out of the 1-14 when I'd left him on his student enrollment (1-10)". Ra seemed confused so he began to explain that I had taught him. I interjected and asked Dumbass, "So you don't remember that morning when I came to you and asked did you mind if I taught Ra?". He replied, "Yeah, I told you that I would think about it. I never gave you a final answer".

This man looked me directly into my eyes and told me a bold-faced lie. It made me furious because I had detected his covetous ways prior to that day. I was hot-tempered back then so, off of impulse, I screamed on him, "Man, you're a lying ass bitch!". I began making my way towards him to slap him in his face but the other Gods formed a buffer between us. I continued to point my finger at him, threatening to slap him. Thats when C-Wise told me, "Yo Born, there is no profanity allowed in the cipher". Once again, off of impulse, I said, "Man, fuck the cipher!". Then I added, "I'm God. I say whatever I want to say". They had me exasperated to the point where I just walked out of the room.

Later on that day, after I cooled down, I decided that the civilized thing to do was to apologize to the Gods who I didn't mean to offend. I figured that some of them would've taken my words, "fuck the cipher", out of context; just to build a case against me. When I said "fuck the cipher", I said it in the sense of "fuck the cipher as the focal point at that moment". C-Wise had addressed the fact that I had used invectives when I felt like he should've been bombing on Dumbass for lying. C-Wise sided with Dumbass because he was one of his little minions who worshipped the ground that he walked on. I didn't, because C-Wise was not my enlightener. And, furthermore, I already knew the 120 lessons when I met C-Wise.

I apologized to most of the Gods and they all said that they knew that I had only reacted that way because I was upset. The only two people who I didn't apologize to were Dumbass and C-Wise. It turned out that C-Wise had disclosed my escape plans to the cipher when I walked out of the room. I felt betrayed because I had shared that information with him in confidence. From that point on, I stopped attending the ciphers. I continued to apply my lessons and to teach whoever desired to learn from me. Ra got into some trouble and he was moved to another dorm.

Before I met Angie, I was in a relationship with a young black woman named Shaquake. When we became involved, she embraced the teachings of the Gods and Earths. I gave her the name Perfect Peace Earth, and she learned the 120 degree lessons, verbatim, in approximately six months. She was a demure and beautiful woman, and she was really good to me. I didn't truly realize that until after we separated. I took her for granted and ended up losing her, plus a whole lot more. Quite frankly, I didn't even have the wherewithal or the maturity to conduct myself as a true man would have.

After my first year in prison on my 17 year sentence, one day I found myself walking through the hallways of the chapel. There were group photographs on the wall for the annual Christian-based program called Kairos. I began to look at the pictures and I noticed a guy who resembled Shaquake's older brother, named J-Rock. I figured that he was just someone who looked like him because he was free when I had last seen him. Plus, he never struck me as the malefactor type. He was a family man with a solvent job.

A few weeks later, I was in the mess hall and eating the last meal of the day. Thats when I spotted J-Rock walking outside of the cafeteria's window. I left my tray on the table and scurried out of the door to catch him. I called out his name, "Yo, J-Rock". He looked back and squinted his eyes, trying to figure out who I was. I said, "This is Now Born". We met each other at midway and exchanged brotherly hugs, laughing and both surprised to see each other. We told each other why we were incarcerated and how much time we had remaining on our sentences. After talking for only a few minutes, he returned to his dorm and I returned inside of the mess hall.

About one month later, I received a new institutional job and got moved into the same dorm that J-Rock lived in. I was still in a relationship with Angie at the time and I didn't hesitate to tell him about her, or show him pictures of her. I also reminded him that I still had strong feelings for his sister, and I would inquire about her often. She was in a relationship with another guy at the time, supposedly engaged to him. I asked him once or twice if I could write her but he didn't feel comfortable with giving me her address.

That same particular dorm was where I had gotten caught with the escape paraphernalia several months later. When I got released from Lock Up after those six months, another inmate got released with me. We were assigned to separate dorms but we carried our properties in the same cart. Our first stop was at the other inmate's dorm. When I walked inside of his dorm with him, the first person that I spotted was J-Rock standing in the sally port of the building. He had been living in that dorm since he'd recently gotten into some trouble.

J-Rock told me that he had been doing some thinking and that he'd decided to entrust his sister's address to me. He said that he really didn't have a problem with it because he knew how close his sister and I were at one point. He said that he viewed me like a brother, and that he wanted me to teach him the knowledge of self. He didn't give me his sister's address that day. I just reported to my assigned dorm, and thats when I moved into the cell with Ra.

A few months later, J-Rock moved into the same dorm that I was in. We started building everyday, and I began teaching him the 120 lessons. He became proficient with the lessons and he started going by the name "120 Allah". He eventually gave me his sister's address. I wrote her and spilled my heart out to her. Unfortunately, she never replied. It was obvious that she had enmity towards me for the way that I mistreated her when we were together. Truth is, I was just immature at the time and I didn't realize what I was doing, nor what I had. There were so many things that my father didn't teach me about being a man, so I was forced to learn through trial and error.

When I began teaching J-Rock, I explained that it was his choice if he wanted the other Gods in the dorm to know that he was learning the 120 degrees. I warned him that we were classified as a security threat group and that it was probably wisest to fly under the radar. I also warned him that, if the other Gods learned that he was studying the lessons, they would've wanted him to attend their ciphers and hang out with them sometimes. Most of them had already been labeled as members of a security threat group and were frequently harassed by the officers. He decided to keep the other Gods out of his business until he had learned all 120 degrees to the point where he could build about them from his own understanding.

One day, a new face moved into the dorm. His name, I decided not to include in this book either. Lets say that his name was Jackass. I had heard about him through Panama, my cellmate from Lock Up. He said that Jackass was one of those problematic Gods who had a reputation for keeping confusion stirred up. When he walked into the dorm, I overheard someone saying his name and I immediately approached him. I wanted to feel him out for myself. I greeted him, "Peace Lord". He returned the greeting, "Peace". Immediately, from his mannerisms, I could tell that he had some type of mental disorder. He seemed skittish.

There was this other guy in our dorm named Fats. I had known him prior to me going to prison. He liked to hustle, plus he didn't seem like a follower. Most importantly, he seemed to have a normal brain. Eventually, he came to me one day and said that he wanted me to teach him the knowledge of self. Of course, I didn't mind. I gave him all of the same warnings that I had given J-Rock. He also decided not to broadcast his affiliation with the nation. He began calling himself "Father Allah True Savior", or "Father Allah" for short. He didn't elevate as quickly as Ra or J-Rock did because he was always preoccupied with hustling to send money home to his daughter.

One night, I had just finished writing a twenty-page letter to my mother, explaining how the black man is God and my understanding of how the universe was created. My plan was to drop it into the prison's outgoing mailbox on the next morning. I figured that Fats would've enjoyed reading my exegesis so I told him that he could read the letter overnight. He returned the letter to me on the next morning and I mailed it out. Another God named Truth lived next door to Fats and they could talk to each other through the vents in their cells. The letter that I had written to my mother had Fats so fascinated that he decided to discuss it with Truth that night. Truth realized from that disquisition that Fats was learning the 120 lessons. Then, he exposed him to the other Gods and they began questioning him about what he knew. Fats came to me immediately afterwards and told me about it. He didn't like the way that they debriefed him. He felt like they had tried to shake his foundation. I simply said, "I warned you".

One day, Fats approached me and said, "Born, I think that I might've gotten you into some trouble". I wondered, "What could he possibly do to get me in trouble?". He said that Jackass had approached him earlier that day and had asked him a few questions. He said that Fats had no right to call himself Father Allah; and that there was only one man who could bear that title, the man who was born as Clarence Smith. He spearheaded the Nation of Gods and Earths in the 1960's. Jackass asked Fats what the last lesson was that he had memorized. Fats answered him, and then Jackass asked him a question pertaining to a previous lesson. Fats did not know the answer. I told Fats not to worry about me being in any type of trouble. All of the Gods knew that I knew and understood the 120 lessons better than any of them. By then, C-Wise had been transferred to another facility, and all of his minions had completely stopped holding ciphers and civilization classes.

C-Wise and I crossed paths about four years later at another prison. We built like men about our differences and I decided to bury the hatchet. We both realized that we were powerful brothers and that our overall cause wasn't personal. We are still friends until this day. I told Fats that Father Allah was a beautiful name and that I had no problem with him choosing it for himself. I said that Clarence 13X (born Clarence Smith) didn't refer to himself as Father Allah. He simply called himself Allah. He was called "The Father" by other Gods who viewed him as a father figure, because he was the only father that some of them had ever known. One God who I remember from Allah School in Mecca, named C-Allah, simply referred to him as "Dad". The Father taught that the black man is God and that his proper name is Allah, which is spelled out by his bodily extremities: Arm-Leg-Leg-Arm-Head. He didn't teach that we should worship him, but that we ourselves were Gods and had the potential to be even greater than him.

My personal mentor at Allah School in Mecca was a man named God Amar Allah. When he taught me the knowledge of self, the first steps were for me to learn the Supreme Mathematics and the Supreme Alphabets. Once I did that, I graduated to 120 degrees. I was taught, by Amar, to learn each degree verbatim first, then do the research. He would say, "First you get the knowledge, then you get the wisdom, then you get the understanding". He said that physical lessons wouldn't always be accessible to me, so I should've memorized them while they were. He said that once I stored them in my attic, or my universal storehouse which is the mind, no one could take them from me. The understanding would come later. Whenever I had questions concerning a particular degree, he'd provide me with his divine understanding and recommend literature for me to read in order to grow my own understanding. He taught me that, "Your own understanding is the best understanding".

When I developed my own understanding and became qualified to teach 120 degrees, I usually used a method that was akin to Amar's. Like, when I had first decided to carry the name "Now Born Allah". I told him, hoping for his stamp of approval, and his exact response was, "Thats a beautiful name, God". At Allah School, there used to be a bumper sticker on the entrance door that read, "One word can change a nation". Amar and all of the older Gods who were fixtures at the school always emphasized the importance of memorizing the lessons word for word, right and exact. One mistaken word could distort the interpretation of the degree. About one year after I went under the tutelage of Amar, he returned to the essence. Before he transcended, he'd entrusted the entire 120 degrees to me, advising me not to cheat myself by studying degrees that I hadn't elevated to. Maybe Amar knew that he would've been leaving the Earth soon. I knew how important it was to him that I learned my degrees right and exact.

The way that Jackass just took license to question my method of teaching made me confront him. Fats and I found Jackass, and I asked him what the problem was. He said that Fats couldn't call himself Father Allah, then I explained why he could. I said that Jackass was being religious and that I knew multiple Gods with Father and Allah in their names. Then he argued that Fats had no business reciting the 4th degree in the 1-14 when he didn't know everything there was to know about the 3rd degree. Fats had memorized the 3rd degree, but had not researched it enough to expound on it adequately. Thats when I asked Jackass, "So, what lesson are you on?". He said that he had mastered all 120 degrees. The 1-14's lesson for that date was about Yacub, so I asked Jackass, "Who was Jacob's father?". He blurted out, "Adam". I said, "No, Isaac". Then I asked, "Who was his mother?". He didn't know so I answered for him, "Rebekah".

I said, "See, you just contradicted yourself. You just did exactly what you accused Fats of doing". The only difference was that Fats wasn't lip-professing like some charlatan who claimed to have mastered 120 degrees. By that point, a few other Gods had approached us and they all witnessed the way that I had disproved Jackass' supposition. We all dispersed and I could tell that Jackass was harboring some hard feelings, simply because he was embarrassed.

Fats came to me again that week. He said that the Gods told him that the way I was teaching him was improper and that if he wanted to continue to learn, he had to learn from them. I noticed that they had planted fear in him because he started saying things like, "I might tell them that they can teach me, but still get my degrees from you on the low". When I realized that he wasn't man enough to just tell the truth and stand firm upon his square, I began to think that he wasn't qualified to carry the name of God. Thats when I started gradually pulling away from him. I didn't want to be held responsible for bringing a weak God into the fold. I couldn't disgrace Amar's name like that, nor my own. My predilection was independent thinkers who were intrepid, as well as studious. Later on that day, I saw the Gods holding a cipher and Fats was in the center, being questioned by all of them. I walked past them and overheard Fats say, "Since Born is teaching me wrong, I want y'all to teach me the right way".

Hours later, I was in my cell, hand-washing my laundry in the sink. Two of the Gods came to my door and said, "We came to notify you that there's been a unanimous decision that you be exiled from the Nation of Gods and Earths". Then I laughed and asked, "Gods and Earths? You niggas aint Gods. Who are you to exile me? I'm the genuine article, not y'all. I was never a part of that fake shit that you have going on anyway. Tell whoever sent you that I said fuck 'em". Then one of them asked, "So, are you gonna continue to teach 120?". My reply was, "Damn right".

I knew that I had just opened up a can of worms with those words but I was disgusted because their hatred towards me had reached such a high pitch. Still, I felt shielded because of my righteousness; even though I was outnumbered. I finished washing my laundry and walked out of my cell about one hour later. Thats when I noticed Fats talking to one of the guys who were at my door. I was receiving cold stares from all of the Gods so I knew that they were planning on doing me some type of physical harm as soon as the c.o. left off of the wing. I didn't clique up with anyone, nor try to find a knife. This one particular Bible verse just kept reverberating in my head, "No weapon formed against me shall prosper".

After a while, the c.o. made an announcement for everyone to go to dinner. Thats when he opened the wing door to release the dorm, and returned to his desk in the center of the pod. I noticed all of the Gods assembling and preparing to leave the building together. On the opposite side of the wing door was a small area called the sally port. The sally port led to the yard. I figured that they were going to be waiting for me in the sally port but I was uncertain. I had opted to go to dinner so I made my way to the door, walking alone. When I reached the door, I saw 8 or 9 of the Gods waiting for me in the sally port. One God was on his way to the yard and I overheard him tell the others, "Don't do it without me". I noticed them and they noticed me. It was clear that they were all functioning at the behest of Jackass.

Only a fool would've entered the sally port unarmed, so I made a u-turn to find a knife and arm myself. I walked past my cellmate, this older black guy named Skee. He was my right-hand man, even though he didn't have knowledge of self. He could tell by the expression on my face that something was wrong, plus he already knew about the beef that was stewing between the Gods and myself. He asked, "Whats going on, Born? You're not going to chow?". I answered, "Nah...those cowards are in the sally port waiting to jump me". Skee said, "Fuck them niggas Born. I ain't no God but I got your back bro".

When we walked into the sally port together, we were flanked by Gods on both sides. They had been waiting for me. My intuition told me to keep my eyes on Jackass. He was waiting on the right side of the door as soon as I walked out. I walked past him and I was about to make my way past the rest of them. I kept Jackass in my peripheral view while watching everyone else simultaneously. I knew that Jackass was the master puppeteer and that the other Gods were his marionettes. Suddenly, I spotted Jackass swinging an object at my head from behind me, and I weaved the blow. When I turned around, he was putting the weapon back into his coat pocket. He had a metal Masterlock tied onto the end of a sock, and had just swung it at me. He ordered the others, "Grab him!". I began backing out of the building with my fists cuffed, daring either one of them to touch me. I threatened Jackass, saying that I was going to thrash him when I caught him by himself. No one touched me or Skee, and we walked to the mess hall together.

When I returned to the dorm, Skee was nowhere to be found. As soon as I entered the building, some guy whispered to me, "Be on point, I just saw Jackass grab a knife". I walked back onto the pod and Jackass was cliqued up with some guys from his hometown. None of them had knowledge of self. He yelled out, "Are you ready to finish what we started?". Then he removed his shirt, inviting me to fight with him in the muslim prayer room. I said, "Let one of my people pat you down and one of yours can pat me down. Then I'll go upstairs and beat the brakes off you". He said, "Ain't nobody patting me down. Come on upstairs". I remained downstairs, knowing that I wouldn't have gotten a fair round. As soon as I would've entered the muslim prayer room, the other Gods and maybe even his homeboys would've filtered in and tried to destroy me. I just posted up by my cell until the c.o. opened my door during his next round. Then, I retired to my cell until the next day.

That next morning, the tension was still thick in the air. Still, I came out of my cell. By afternoon, Gods who I'd never met had came from other dorms and they were holding a big cipher in the Phone Room. It didn't take a rocket scientist to know that they were talking about destroying me. There were at least 25 Gods in the Phone Room. For my own safety, I told someone to go to the Phone Room and tell one of the ring-leaders to come and speak to me alone. Momentarily, he came out and approached me by himself. When he approached me, I folded my arms and asked, "Whats the Gods' case against me?". First, he said that I had went behind Dumbass' back and had stolen his student. I told him what truly happened concerning that, and then he raised his next claim - that I had given Fats the name Father Allah to be controversial. I said that Fats had chosen that name for himself, and that his full name was Father Allah True Saviour, an acronym for Fats. Then, I explained the incident when I had said, "Fuck the cipher".

Other Gods began to emerge from the Phone Room and, before I knew it, they had all coalesced around me. Most of them had heard my rebuttal. Suddenly, Jackass interjected like he was ready for some action. He said, "Man, fuck all of this. I just wanna ask Born one thing. Born...are you gonna continue teaching 120?". I believed that if I would've said yes, one of them would've swung on me and the others would've followed suit. I hesitated for a moment, then I answered, "Yeah". My mother didn't raise a coward and, at that point, I was ready to get mashed out. Surprisingly, Jackass said, "Well, I think that he should keep teaching because the God is true and living in my eyes. That beef is between him and C-Wise and we all know that. Born was the first God to say "Peace" to me when I moved into this dorm. Plus, yesterday he bombed me and made me go back into the lab to study all night long. I don't have a problem with Born. I'm out of it". Then he extended his arm to shake my hand.

I extended an olive branch to him by shaking his hand although the idea that simmered in the back of my mind was, "That was righteous but I'm still gonna work you out for swinging that Masterlock at me". After Jackass walked away, most of the other Gods said, "Yeah, I'm out of it too. This ain't right and exact". Only a few of them couldn't admit to being wrong. Their inferiority complexes wouldn't allow it. They just walked away and left me standing alone. After the smoke had cleared, Fats decided to approach me with a smile on his face. He said something like, "I told you that we would be victorious, God". I just turned and walked away. A few years later, Jackass joined the Black Gangster Disciples. It didn't surprise me at all.

13

THE BOILING POINT

There used to be this one black guy who lived in the cell next door to me. At the time, the white guy named Jett was my cellmate. Lets say that this guy's name was Chill. Chill and I could speak to each other through the vents in our cells. We began conversing almost daily after I learned that he was from my ex-earth, Shaquake's, hometown. He was surprised to know that I knew people from his hometown, and was familiar with the area. I had never heard of that town prior to meeting Shaquake. When she and I became involved, I began hanging out in that town with her. Eventually, I ended up violating my parole and going on the run. Thats when I practically moved to that town, and hid out in a local motel for a few months.

During that time, I learned almost everything that there was to know about that town. I was hustling and had established some new clientele there. After seeing the photos in Chill's photo album, I learned that he'd been dealing with a female who I had my eyes on when I was in his town. I never actually pursued her but, judging from the few times that we crossed paths, she would've given me a chance if I would've tried my hand. Chill did link me back up with one female from his town. I had met her after Shaquake and I separated. It wasn't anything serious, just a one-night stand type of deal.

Chill and I got pretty cool during the few months that he lived next door to me. For some reason, he ended up moving downstairs; on the opposite end of our pod. He moved into a cell with this black guy who was about ten years older than him. Because of his height, lets say that his name was Too Tall. He struck most inmates as being somewhat bourgeois. I always viewed him as only being aloof from everyone, just as I was with most people. He was the clerk for the dorm Lieutenant so, naturally, he was labeled as a snitch. He had pretty much everything that an inmate was permitted to buy: a tv, a Walkman, new sneakers, new t-shirts, plus he always had money to buy food and hygiene items from the canteen with. Another rumor that was circulating about him was that he was very skilled in Martial Arts.

Chill was different. He didn't have much. When he moved into Too Tall's cell, he started complaining to me about how selfish Too Tall was. Too Tall wasn't sharing any of his things with Chill, not even his cellphone. Chill began to feel livid about Too Tall talking on the phone inside of their cell everyday, without offering it to him so that he could reach out. After a while, Chill began intimating to me that he was considering robbing Too Tall. I never took him seriously because I couldn't fathom how a man could rob his cellmate, then continue to sleep around him every night.

Time went on and Chill stopped talking about it. One day, everyone was locked in their cells for 12:30 count-time. Suddenly, someone downstairs began kicking on their cell door as hard as they could. Normally, when that happens, an inmate is trying to alarm the dorm officer that their cellmate has just committed suicide, or had died somehow. A lot of times, inmates pretend like there's an emergency, just to get the officer to come to their cells as a prank. When I heard the banging on the door, thats what I assumed the case was. I heard the c.o. respond to the inmate downstairs, "What do you want?". Then I heard the inmate answer, "Come to my door! Its an emergency! Hurry up!". The officer must've also believed that it was a prank because he walked to the man's cell as slowly as he could. By the time that he arrived at his door, he was out of my view so I had walked away from the door.

A few seconds later, I heard the sound of a cell door being opened. Then, what sounded like someone running up the stairs. Usually, during count-time, the entire dorm was silent. So, the sound of someone running up the stairs was definitely out of the ordinary. I walked back to my cell door and began looking out of the window to see who had ran out of his cell in the middle of count-time. It wasn't long before I saw Too Tall speeding past my cell. His shirt was off and most of his skin had been removed from his back, his left side, and the left side of his chest. He had obviously been burned. He was yelling like mad, straining his muscles and gritting his teeth. At one point, he dropped to his knees and began to yell even louder. By then, everyone was staring out of their windows at Too Tall as he kneeled in the center of the pod and winced in pain.

A few nurses entered the dorm to escort him to the medical building, which was about a three minute walk away. I didn't have a window view of the front of our dorm, but a few of my partners did. It was a hot and sunny day. They said that Too Tall went haywire when the sunrays hit his back. He ran nonstop to the medical building, yelling every step of the way. Shortly afterwards, a few Lieutenants came through the entrance door and placed Chill into handcuffs. Then, they escorted him to Lock Up where he remained for several months.

It turned out that Chill had finally tried to rob Too Tall in their cell that day. Chill had pulled out an improvised ice pick and threatened that he would stab Too Tall if he didn't hand over his cellphone. They were locked inside of their cell. Therefore, Chill couldn't go anywhere after the robbery. Too Tall decided to call his bluff and they began fighting. The people who lived next door to them said that it sounded like Too Tall was getting the best of Chill. For the entire time that they were in their cell, Chill had his coffee pot plugged into the wall, boiling some water mixed with baby oil. Too Tall assumed that Chill was simply boiling water to cook some food with. In the middle of the fight, Chill grabbed the coffee pot and doused the boiling water on Too Tall from the side of him. Luckily, the water didn't contact his face. His upper torso was burned severely. His first reaction was to remove his shirt. When he did, his skin came off with it.

Surprisingly, our dorm didn't get locked down because of that incident. I guess thats because it was an isolated incident, and both of the parties involved were taken out of the dorm. As soon as the count cleared, the officer began opening our cell doors. Of course, that incident was the topic of everyone's discussion. The first thing that I noticed was that there was a ball of Too Tall's skin on the floor, directly in front of my cell. Obviously, that skin had melted off of him and dripped onto the floor as he sped past my door. I never saw Too Tall again after that day. Chill was eventually reposited into general population, and I would still see him from time to time. When I asked him about the above incident, he seemed to find it quite comical.

14

THE DRUNKEN CELLMATE

When I was being housed in the so-called honor dorm, I didn't befriend many people. I moved reticently because I didn't know many people, and I was still fresh on my 17 year bid. I would sometimes talk to J-Rock, my partner named Divine, and this older guy. Lets say that the older guy's name was Paulie. Paulie was a real stand-up guy, and it was obvious that he was about his money prior to his incarceration. He was an astute businessman. I actually used to call him "Uncle Paulie" because he reminded me of Uncle Paulie from the movie Goodfellas. He was black but he moved like one of those Italian mob bosses. He was sort of chubby, rarely seen, and he didn't interact with many people. He would cover his mouth whenever he spoke to me while people were around.

He didn't want people to read his lips because he was really clandestine about his business.

A lot of people looked up to Paulie, mainly because of his money. He wasn't selfish, nor was he a pushover. He was the type of person that you wouldn't want to burn your bridge with. You definitely would've needed him again before he needed you. When I met Paulie, there weren't many cellphones in the prison. Only the elite few had them and they were very secretive about them. Back then, you would be sent to Lock Up if the officers even suspected that you had one. Over time, they became more plentiful and the penalties became less harsh.

Paulie took a liking to me for some reason. I would politic with him in his cell for hours sometimes, soaking up the game on how to make money in the pen like him. He would lend his cellphone to me often, and he would entrust confidential information to me about buisness that he had going on. He wasn't in the Nation of Gods and Earths, but I still had reverence for him. In fact, during that time, I was going through my Christianity phase.

Paulie had a lot of people who would come around, suckling at the power teat. Most of them didn't have his best interest at heart and I'm sure that he realized that. He wasn't a slow leak at all. For some reason, after only knowing him for a short while, I was willing to defend him from anyone who wanted to harm him. In retrospect now, as petty as it sounds, that reason was probably because he allowed me to call Angie on his cellphone everyday.

On this one particular day, I returned to my dorm after a grueling day at work in the cafeteria. After I took my shower, I walked over to Paulie's pod to build with him like I normally would. The dorm was divided into four pods: A pod, B pod, C pod and D pod. The dorm was designed in the shape of a horseshoe. In the center of the dorm was a station that we called the O.P., which stood for "Officers' Post". The honor dorm was larger than all of the other dorms so there were always at least two officers in the O.P. at a time. From the O.P., the officers could monitor what went on in each one of the pods.

When I entered Paulie's pod, I noticed that he seemed dejected for some reason. When I asked what the problem was, he told me that he was having problems with this white guy in our dorm. The white guy was who Paulie always paid to stash his cellphone whenever the contraband search team would come and do mass shakedowns. The white guy had told Paulie that the contraband team had found Paulie's phone in his stash spot. Somehow, Paulie learned that he had lied. When I entered the cell, Paulie was still deciding on what to do about the situation. My partner named Divine was also present in the cell. He and I had agreed to go and thrash the white guy for Paulie. We knew that he would've never saw it coming. Paulie just told us to relax. The white guy was on his way to Paulie's cell to state his case and come to an agreement on how Paulie would be reimbursed.

A few seconds later, there was a knock on the door. Paulie said, "Come in". Then, the cell door slid open. An older black guy from C pod entered the cell first, and the white guy walked in behind him. They allowed the door to shut behind themselves and the white guy planted his back against it. He stood quietly as the black guy did all of the speaking for him. He argued vehemently, "Look, this white boy is my homeboy and I've been knowing him for years! He ain't gotta steal shit! Ain't nobody gonna put their hands on this white boy!". I don't know if they were homo lovers or what, but the black guy was obviously drunk. I was sitting on top of Paulie's cooler, on the floor. As the black guy was mouthing off, I looked over at the white guy. Thats when I noticed that he was clutching the handle of a knife with his right hand. The blade was cloaked by the sleeve of his thermal shirt.

I gave Paulie an eye signal, letting him know that the white guy was carrying. He allowed the black guy to babble on, still maintaining his poise. Then, he gave Divine and I a look to stand down. I didn't know any history on these two men but, for some reason, Paulie didn't want the situation to escalate. The white guy spoke his piece and promised Paulie his recompense as soon as his family could come up with the cash. He was far less abrasive than his black friend was. Paulie appeared to be satisfied with their arrangement, and he allowed them to leave the cell. As soon as they left, we thought that Paulie was about to tell us to go and stab both of them up. In my green mind, I probably would've done it. Strangely, Paulie just dismissed the situation like it was nothing.

Less than one month later, I was walking around inside of B pod one night. The wing doors to each pod were locked because it was time for the 7:30 institutional count. The count procedure was unique in the honor dorm because we were allowed to walk around inside of our assigned pods. All other times of the day, we could bounce from one pod to another. From B pod, I could look directly into C pod, depending on which section of B pod I was standing in. I noticed that the officer had opened the wing door for C pod, allowing an inmate to approach the O.P.'s window. I couldn't tell what he was saying to the female officer. All I knew was that she just blew him off and made him return to his pod. Then both officers began walking from pod to pod, to conduct their counts. They were both black women in their late twenties.

Whenever the officers came into our pod to count us, we had to stand beside the cells that we were assigned to. On their way out of the pod, they would announce, "As you were". Then we were allowed to resume doing whatever we were doing prior to the count. After the count, I looked over at the O.P. and one of the female officers was inside, pacing frantically. She seemed to be traumatized at something. Then, I heard the First Response call being made over the intercom, urging that the First Response team reported to our dorm immediately. Shortly afterwards, a second announcement was made over the intercom. That time, they called for medical assistance in our dorm.

Realizing that nothing had happened in B pod, I walked over to the window to see if something was happening inside of C pod. Thats when I spotted a black man sprawled across the floor with blood spilling from his head. He wasn't moving and everyone in C pod was just standing around, staring at him. The nurses and the hospice workers rushed into the dorm a few minutes later. Then, they rushed into C pod. By then, every inmate in B pod was standing at the window; waiting to see who was about to be carried out on the stretcher.

There were two entrance doors in that dorm. One door led to A pod and B pod. The second door led to C pod and D pod. If the hospice workers would've carried the man out of the second door, I wouldn't have been able to see who was on the stretcher. They decided to carry the man out of the dorm, through the door that was closest to A pod and B pod. We all stared as they walked past the window. Thats when I realized that the man on the stretcher was the black guy who had came into Paulie's cell to defend the white guy. At first sight, I knew that he was dead because his eyes were opened wide and they weren't moving.

That was the first time that I had ever seen a dead man in prison. I later found out what had happened. The victim was drunk, as he normally was. He and his cellmate had gotten into an argument. He threatened his cellmate, saying that if he came into their cell that night, he was going to stab him to death. His cellmate tried to curtail the situation by asking a dorm officer to put him in a different cell for the night. She didn't take him seriously. Instead, she told him to return to his pod. Thats what was happening when I had seen him approach the O.P.'s window during count-time that night..

When he returned to his pod, the man still continued to threaten him. Then, the drunk man decided to spit in his face. The cellmate still didn't want to retaliate. He just left the spit trickling down the side of his face for the officer to see it when she came around to count. She saw the spit on his face but still didn't take him seriously. By the time that she returned to the O.P., the drunk man's cellmate had reached his wits' end. Thats when he walked over to the storage closet and retrieved a push broom. Then he unscrewed the handle and grabbed the bottom part of the broom, where the bristles were.

The bristles were made into a 2X4" board that was about 2.5 feet long. He crept up on his drunken cellmate and struck him in his temple with the board. That one single blow ended him. The officer actually witnessed the blow and thats what caused her to pace frantically inside of the O.P. that night. The man who killed his cellmate was taken to Lock Up and indicted for murder. Somehow, he beat the charge. I'm not sure about how he did it because the state that we were in doesn't have a self-defense statute. The officer who denied him a cell change that night was fired. The irony of it all was that the man who died only had two weeks remaining before his release date.

15

THE EASY WAY OUT

The picture on the previous page was taken by an inmate who lived in a different dorm from the one that I lived in. The image was forwarded to my cellmate's cellphone. About one week earlier, we had heard about some white guy who had committed suicide in another dorm. The inmate who snapped the photo on his cellphone happened to live in that very dorm, and had witnessed the incident. He took the picture from inside of his cell, through the window on his door. He decided to forward it to several inmates throughout the prison. Most inmates had lots of other inmates' names and cellphone numbers saved into their cellphones' contacts, for various reasons. A lot of people who were involved in the illegal business that went on liked to network with inmates in other dorms. Guys who had a view of the staff's parking lot from their cell windows would send out mass text messages, warning their partners whenever the contraband search team was pulling into the parking lot.

Me personally, I never saved other inmates' cellphone numbers in my contacts. Nor did I give out my number. Oftentimes, when inmates would get caught with cellphones, the officers would learn what other inmates had phones by going through their call logs and their contacts. The man in the photograph was a caucasian man who was in his early 40's. He lived in a dorm where the majority of the inmates were considered as mental health patients. Only about 10% of the men in that dorm were normal. They were just on special medications because of physical health problems. The caucasian man had decided to attempt suicide for reasons that are beyond me. All I know is that one morning around 11:00 a.m., he walked up to the top tier in his pod and tied a blindfold over his eyes. Then he swan-dived headfirst over the rail, with his hands down by his side. The bottom floor was made of pure concrete beneath the floor tiles, and it was a 12 foot drop from the top tier.

Witnesses said that the man hit the floor headfirst and that his head split like a melon upon contact. They heard his skull crack and the blood began pouring out profusely. Indubitably, he died as soon as his head hit the floor. Whenever a murder occurs in a dorm, the entire prison goes on lockdown status for a few days. Since this was a suicide case, that particular dorm was the only dorm to be locked down and they only remained locked down for two or three days. That was how long it took for the Crime Scene Investigators to wrap-up their investigation.

During that time, I was frequently posting different status updates on Facebook. I decided to share that photo one day. Right above it, I captioned, "I tried to tell people that its real in here. This guy couldn't take it so he bodied himself". I didn't share the photo to gross people out. I mainly did it to show some of my family members and friends that some people in my same predicament weren't strong enough to endure what I did on a daily basis. Some people went stir crazy or got strung out on mental health medication. Some people ended up killing other inmates, and some simply committed suicide. A lot of those people who I tried to illustrate that point to, at the time, seemed to be turning their backs on me or writing me off.

In prison, sometimes thats actually the case. Other times, you're probably just being hypersensitive. The responses that I got from most people on Facebook were, "Wow", "Thats crass", or "Thats crazy". Some of my Facebook friends didn't know me personally, so they probably just assumed that I was sharing a photo that I had downloaded from online. Until this day, I still have that picture saved into my "Mobile Uploads" photo album on Facebook.

16

UNJUST DON'T PROSPER

When I got sentenced to 17 years, I was classified as a violent offender. Therefore, I wasn't eligible for parole until I had completed 85% of that time. That would've been approximately 14 years and 8 months. I would've had to serve the entire 17 years if I had refused to accept an institutional job assignment. I had a number of different jobs while incarcerated. I worked in the cafeteria. I worked for the Prison Industries, and I've worked as a ward keeper; to name a few.

The most lax job that I ever had while in prison was in the prison's general library. In the library, my job was simple. I was in charge of periodicals. All I did was issue out magazines and newspapers to the inmates, and made sure that they were returned before those inmates left the library. I had a large wooden desk where I had privacy to write my letters, read books, and study legal material with minimal distraction from anyone. Thats how most of my days were spent at work.

I worked in Periodicals alone for a few months, then the Librarian hired another guy to work with me. His name was Gregg, but I just called him "G". He was serving a life sentence. He wasn't a distraction at all because he was always busy studying his case, trying to get back into court. Gregg was about 15 years older than I was but we became good friends. He asked me to teach him the 120 lessons so I began teaching him. He was actually the oldest person who I'd ever taught the lessons to. He had came in contact with the lessons over 15 years before we had met, but he had abandoned them for some reason. Subsequent to meeting me, he decided that he needed to learn them again and begin applying them to his everyday life.

Another good friend that I met in the library was a man named Tyson. He was also serving a life sentence. He was about twenty years older than I was. Tyson and I had a few things in common. He was a singer and a musician, plus he had already published a book. During that time, I was still trying to publish my first book. He gave me a few pointers on how I should've went about doing it, even though I went an entirely different route. I also met another guy who worked in the library. Lets just say that his name was A.B. He was about 15 years older than I was. He was serving a 30 year sentence. At first, I barely even noticed that he was working in the library because he was always sequestered in a small office in the back. He had some idiosyncrasies about himself that made him seem conspicuous. I later found out that he was affiliated with the inmates who smuggled most of the contraband into the prison. I ended up buying a cellphone from him. The deal went smooth so I assumed that he always did good business.

After a while, A.B. and I got pretty cool. After building with me, he took notice of the fact that I had somewhat of a revolutionary spirit. Thats when he confided to me that he was planning to escape, and that I was welcome to tag along if I was interested. Given his personality, I initially took what he said with a grain of salt. At the same time, escaping was right up my alley so I heard him out. His plan didn't sound all that fool-proof but it did have some perks that my first plan didn't have. He could get things smuggled in, like drugs and cellphones. With those, we could've hustled up enough cash to pay some people in society to help us to break out. Also, just as easily as he could've gotten drugs and cellphones in, he could've gotten us guns, bolt cutters to cut the fences with, and other tools that would've been conducive to our plans.

So, that was our common thread; the desire to leave by any means necessary. He also allegedly had more outside help than I did. Pretty soon, I was going into his office almost daily and discussing the plan with him. This was about two years after I had been released from Lock Up for getting caught with escape paraphernalia. If A.B. and I would've gotten away, we probably would've gotten ourselves killed on the run. Our plan included pulling off a few heists as soon as we escaped. Also, going out in a blaze if the cops ever caught up with us. Going back to prison was out of the question.

One day, I walked into A.B.'s office to build with him about our plans. He didn't feel like discussing them because he had something on his mind. I noticed that he had a Gemstar razor blade on his desk. That was the first Gemstar that I had seen since I'd been in prison. I was only used to seeing what we called "bangers". When I was home, I called Gemstars "bangers" too. But, at that particular prison, bangers were improvised knives that were made from any type of scrap metal that the inmates could find. Most of the knives were either flat blades or ice picks. A.B. told me that he was carrying that razor blade around because someone had been threatening to stab him. I didn't think that a razor blade would've been much of a match for a knife. In my opinion, a stabbing would've been a lot worse than a cut across the face.

I asked A.B. what the beef was about and he said that he had sold the guy a cell phone for $400. The guy complained that the phone didn't work and that he wanted a refund. I suggested that A.B. just gave the guy back his money in exchange for the phone. Cellphones are a hot commodity in prison, and the phone would've resold in no time. A.B. said that he wasn't going to refund the man because he was lying. His reason sounded suspect to me and, from the glare in his eyes, I could tell that there was some underhanded activity involved. I assumed that he had deliberately sold the guy a damaged phone and had already spent the money. At that time, I didn't know who the other guy was.

As I mentioned earlier, from day one, I'd always felt like A.B. had an air of suspiciousness about himself. After he told me about that cellphone situation, I started second-guessing the escape plans that we had made. I believed that he was probably lying about everything else because he never really showed me any proof besides a few cellphones, digital scales and weed. He could've been a liaison, simply trafficking for a small cut.

I told him that day in his office that he probably didn't have anything to worry about, especially since he had said that the guy was a younger man in his early twenties. A.B. was at least 45 years-old. For the remainder of that day, I kept my mouth shut about everything that we had discussed in that office. None of the other library workers knew that A.B. had a beef pending. Around 4:30 that afternoon, the 3:30 count cleared and we were all released from work. We were supposed to report back to our assigned dorms but all of the library workers normally went directly to the mess hall after work. After the 3:30 count cleared was when the cafeteria always began feeding dinner to every dorm. The prison fed all of the inmates, one dorm at a time. A.B. and I lived in separate dorms, but we all proceeded to the mess hall anyway.

I was actually walking with Gregg. A.B. was lagging a few feet behind us, walking by himself. Once inside of the mess hall, Gregg and I walked through the serving line and received our dinner trays. Then we sat at the same table together. There weren't many other inmates in the mess hall at the time, only about 15 library/education workers. The cafeteria hadn't begun feeding the first dorm yet. There was only one officer in the mess hall, a young black female. Plus, there were a few cafeteria workers hanging around.

I was eating my food while Gregg was talking to me about something. The officer walked out of the mess hall and onto the yard. The library workers were basically viewed as model inmates, so she probably had assumed that we didn't need any supervision. Suddenly, Gregg and I heard what sounded like a loud clap, "Papp!". We looked into the direction of the sound, and thats when we noticed A.B. stumbling to the floor. This young guy had just punched him in his face. Immediately, I concluded that he was the same guy who A.B. had told me about earlier that day.

The blow had stunned A.B. for a moment. When he snapped out of it, he reached for the razor blade that was in his sock; while attempting to stand up. Thats when the guy rushed over to him while pulling a long and shiny ice pick from his waistband. Then he asked, "Oh...you're getting up?". A.B. threw up his right arm and tried to block it but the guy began stabbing him in his triceps and his shoulder. A.B. yelled each time that the knife penetrated him, three times totaled. It was obvious that he was not trying to kill A.B., but only sending warning shots to scare him. A.B. was on the floor crying, "Okay man, don't kill me". Then the guy demanded, "Get my fuckin' money". A.B. acquiesced, "Okay", with his eyes fraught with tears. He looked terrified.

The guy allowed A.B. to stand up while he still had the ice pick exposed, in clear view to all of us. A.B. seemed to be hesitating to walk out of the door, as if he was contemplating on retaliation. The guy began rushing towards him again, threatening, "Do you want some more nigga!?". A.B. began to put some pep in his step, crying, "No bruh...I'mma get your money man. I'mma get your money". Thats when A.B. walked out of the mess hall and returned to his dorm. The young guy sheathed his knife in his pants and returned to work on the serving line like nothing had happened. If I didn't know any better, I would've believed that the female officer was in cahoots with him. It was just peculiar how she was walking back into the cafeteria just as A.B. was walking out of a different door. She didn't witness anything. She didn't even notice A.B. walking back to his dorm and holding his arm because of his stab wounds.

Seeing A.B. get stabbed up had spoiled my appetite for that entire evening. Even though he did misappropriate that man's funds, I still didn't want to see him get stabbed up like that. I knew that he was embarrassed because of the way that everything had went down. He'd practically gotten knocked out by a kid who was almost half of his age. The next day at work was awkwardly silent. Everyone had witnessed the incident and was sort of disturbed by it. I was almost certain that A.B. was going to admit himself into Protective Custody, especially after I learned that the young guy was a gang member.

This one white guy who lived in A.B.'s dorm told us that A.B. was still living in the dorm a few days later. He had decided not to go into Protective Custody. He didn't even go to the nurses to get stitched up. Instead, some white guy had stitched him up with a needle and some thread. I don't know if A.B. ever cleared his debt because he never returned to work in the library. Therefore, all of our escape plans went south. I know now that this was a blessing in disguise. The last news that I heard about A.B. was that he'd gotten caught with some contraband and was taken to Lock Up. I haven't seen him since the day of his stabbing.

17

THE GANG EPIDEMIC

Another growing epidemic in the prisons is the gang violence. A lot of the inmates were members of various gangs prior to going to prison. Others got initiated while incarcerated. I would notice the way that the gangs would practically go around giving out draft notices and seeking recruits to increase their numbers. The majority of the gang members were young black men in their early twenties. There were a few older members, and they were dubbed as the "Big homies". Most of them had been in prison for many years so they had seniority in their gangs. They sometimes had pull with the officers as well. Rarely, I would see older men joining these gangs. Whenever I did, I always viewed them as simply trying to feel young again. They seemed retrograde in my opinion.

My overall take on the whole gang business was that it was just a bunch of young brothers following a popular trend. I would notice how the new arrivals would come to prison, and the gangs would immediately start trying to figure out which gang they belonged to. A lot of the new arrivals would be young brothers with a lot of time, often life sentences. Most of them looked deathly afraid when they walked through the doors for the first time. Almost naturally, they began searching for a group to join for protective concerns. I can recall when this one younger brother had first came through the doors. He looked scared to death. He was a neutral, meaning that he didn't belong to any gang, nor organization. Over time, I would see him talking to this person and that person. It was obvious that he was malleable and looking for a group to join.

Someone must've told this young guy that I was in the Nation of Gods and Earths. One day, I was standing near the Phone Room alone. He came and stood next to me, but he remained silent for a second. Next, he tried to initiate a conversation with me by saying, "Ayo, I don't believe in God man". I looked at him askance and asked, "What type of way is that to approach a perfect stranger?". He replied, "I'm just saying...I believe that I'm God". I simply said, "Thats whats up". Then, I walked away. As I said in Chapter Six, I dislike it when people are implicit, instead of being direct. Therefore, I kept my distance from him. In a matter of two weeks, he was a part of a gang. After he joined, I watched him transition from a quiet little snail to a silverback gorilla. Now under the auspices of that gang, he started pretending like he had heart. Thats generally the case when young brothers join gangs in prison. They try to overcompensate for their cowardice by taking on gangster names and rolling in packs.

They normally gravitate towards the gang that is the most dominant in the dorm that they are living in, meaning the gang with the most members. The rappers in the music industry seem to have a heavy influence on these young brothers who are joining these gangs. I later became acquainted with the young brother who I mentioned in the previous paragraph. I remember asking him once, "What made you join that gang?". His answer was, "It was because of the knowledge". I asked, "What knowledge?". First, he told me a few trite phrases that had been around for years, like "death before dishonor" and "real recognizes real". Apparently, he wasn't learning any exclusive information in his gang.

Most of the gangs looked at the Gods as the ones who possessed the proper knowledge. I've seen some gang sets even study lessons that were carbon copies of the Gods' lessons. One Folk (Gangster Disciple) member told me that he was studying a Folk lesson called the "5 Stages of a G Mind". When he quoted it to me, it was almost identical to a plus lesson thats been with the Nation of Gods and Earths for decades, known as the "5 Stages of Consciousness". I also met a Bloodmember who showed me his set's alphabetical system on paper, and it was a facsimile of the Gods and Earths' Supreme Alphabets.

Most of the gangs claim to be revolutionaries. The members who do study, often read literature about George L. Jackson, Assada Shakur, the Black Panther Party, and etc. They also have revolutionary acronyms for their gang titles. Blood is supposed to stand for Black Leaders Of Our Day, or Black Leaders Out of Oppression and Depression. Crip is supposed to stand for Community Revolution In Progress. The Folks use the term BOS, which is supposed to stand for Brothers Of the Struggle. I always viewed those names as misnomers because the revolutionary element suffers in most of the gangs. However, I have met a handful of gangmembers who were truly dedicated to their revolutionary cause. They were usually the brains in the outfit. The Bloods and Crips don't allow white people to join them. The Folks do have one particular branch that accepts white members. Its called I.G.D., the initials for Insane Gangster Disciples.

What always bewildered me about white members joining their ranks was the fact that they still proclaimed to be revolutionaries. I've seen cases when white members had authority over black members. All of the revolutionaries, who the gangs claim to pattern themselves after, fought against the social conditions that had been bestowed upon us by the white race. They challenged issues like white supremacy, fascism, imperialism, capitalism, and racial discrimination. In my opinion, allowing whites into a black revolutionary movement would seem both toxic and contradictory to their overall revolutionary cause. But, thats just my opinion.

I was told by an elder that before the gangs began to permeate the prisons, most of the black youths gravitated towards the Gods and Earths, the Rastafarians, and the Nation of Islam. Then came along the practice of Al-Islam. Al-Islam allows white people to come under the banner of Islam. So, now its very commonplace to meet caucasians in prison with names like Muhammed, Rahim, or Aziz. Most of them join the religion for protective purposes, and still remain racists behind closed doors.

This one guy who I will probably always remember was a young Folk member, about twenty years of age. His visage was like that of a young teenager. Lets say that his name was "Little G". I can recall the day when he first walked through the doors as a new arrival. He looked afraid. He seemed reserved, quiet and observant. He had this look about himself like he was from a decent family. Like he probably had a nice girlfriend at home, and maybe a young daughter. Nothing about him said "gangster" or "thug". I never really spoke to Little G because he wasn't in my age bracket. We crossed paths once or twice, but we never really said anything to each other. I soon realized that he was a member of the Folks. He began hanging around some young Folk members who had recently been initiated themselves. They were always grouped up, smoking, drinking, rapping or having trivial debates.

One Friday morning, I was sitting in the barber chair and reading a book. I wasn't getting a haircut. Its just that the barber chair was the only soft chair in the entire dorm. Everyone else had to either sit on the benches, sit on the stairs, or stand up. I needed to walk upstairs to my cell for something and I knew that, as soon as I would've walked away, someone else would've sat down in the barber chair. My intentions were to come right back. Little G happened to be walking by. Thats when I asked him if he would sit in the chair and hold it down for me while I ran upstairs. He obliged so I went up to my cell and returned within two minutes. Then, we bumped fists and I thanked him.

About six hours later, the dorm officer released the dorm to the mess hall for dinner. On my way back from the mess hall, I noticed a few hospice workers leaving our dorm. They were carrying someone on a stretcher, walking in double-time. As soon as I returned to the dorm, we were being placed on lockdown status for a stabbing that had occurred. There was too much pandemonium in the dorm to try and figure out who had done what. I just rushed to get a last-minute shower because I figured that we would've remained on lockdown status for a week or two at best.

When I stepped out of the shower, I learned that Little G was the one who had been stabbed. I didn't find out the entire story until I returned to my cell. My cellmate was in the dorm when the incident transpired and he recapitulated it to me. Before the dorm had gotten released for dinner, the dorm officer had been calling out Little G's government name to notify him that he had a visitor. Normally what happens is that you will hear your name being called. If not, someone who knows you will hear it and let you know that your name was called for a visit. The officer in the visitation room kept calling our dorm officer on the telephone because Little G's visitors were becoming worried about why he hadn't arrived in the visitation room yet. They had been waiting for over thirty minutes.

After receiving the last call from the visitation officer, the dorm officer decided to do the only sensible thing to do. He walked over to Little G's cell to see if he was inside, sleeping. When the officer opened Little G's door, he discovered him lying in his bed, bleeding profusely from multiple stab wounds. He wasn't responding, and the officer believed that he was dead. Thats when he made an emergency First Response call on his Walkie-Talkie radio. Then, the lieutenants and other rescue personnel came to the dorm and carried him to the medical building.

It turned out that Little G had done something that broke his gang's protocol. The disturbing part about the situation was that a white guy in their gang had ordered the hit. He had sent a few black guys to stab up another black kid, and they obeyed him. Little G's mother, his girlfriend and his child were all in the visitation room waiting for him while he was in his bed bleeding to death. If they wouldn't have came to visit him, he definitely would've bled to death because the officer wouldn't have found out about him in time to save his life. I never saw Little G again after that day but the dorm officer told some of the inmates that he had survived a few days later.

A lot of people seemed to feel indignant about the fact that a white man had ordered the hit on a black man. I was upset, although that wasn't my first time seeing a white guy pit blacks against blacks. On the day that we came off of lockdown, a meeting was held in the Muslim Prayer Room. Gods were there, Bloods, Crips, Folks and even Muslims. There was a lot of talk about getting the white guy out of our dorm but nothing ever happened to him. On the night that Little G got stabbed, I had a dream that I had gotten stabbed in my stomach three times. The next morning, my cellmate told me that I had been making sounds like I was about to regurgitate in my sleep. I knew that I had made those sounds each time that I had gotten stabbed in my dream. I must've been thinking about the Little G incident really hard before I had fallen asleep.

18

CRAZY LOVE

I once got transferred from one prison to another because of a reduction in my custody level. When I first arrived there, I didn't know what to expect but I had been anticipating a new scenery. This particular prison was a lot different from my previous institution. It was less violent and the prison operated under controlled movement. I had just left a prison where contraband was plentiful: cellphones, drugs, cigarettes and etc. Immediately, I began searching to find out who was doing what, because I wanted to get connected. I didn't smoke or drink but I had became accustomed to using cellphones in prison. I also wanted to see how I could make some extra cash.

Another thing that was different about this particular prison was the abundance of female staff members. There were some attractive women working there and, if you had any type of magnetic about yourself, they would fraternize and flirt with you. After a few days, I had applied for almost every institutional job, and I had learned almost everything about the economy at that prison. There weren't many cellphones, but drugs and tobacco always seemed to find their ways into the prison. While I was there, there was another growing epidemic known as "K-2". Some people call it "synthetic marijuana" but, from what I understand, its actually some type of potpourri that they smoke and get a much more intense high than they would get from weed; without the risk of failing a urinalysis. I've literally seen inmates temporarily lose their minds after smoking K-2, and I've heard of cases where inmates have died from using it. When K-2 first arrived on the scene, it permeated the prison system like a virulent infection.

The first job to interview me was Food Service. They hired me on the spot because I had previous experience from other prisons. The first thing that I noticed was that the majority of the kitchen supervisors were females. There was one in particular who I became interested in at first sight. She was exceptionally beautiful, plus she seemed really spirited and friendly. All of the other inmates who worked in the cafeteria seemed to favor her above all of the other supervisors. On my first day working with her, she asked me what my name was and I answered, "Born". Almost one hour later, I heard her call out my name. I walked over to see what she wanted and she told me that she had allowed for one of the guys to cook some type of casserole with sausage in it, and that I was welcome to have some. I told her that I would pass because I didn't eat meat. I was already feeling her by then, but I wasn't ready to pursue her yet.

One day, out of the blue, this one guy who worked with me came to me and asked, "Do you see ol' girl right there?", referring to her. I didn't even know him. I answered, "Yeah.

Whats up with her?". He replied, "Thats my chick. You can ask anybody...I got her". I didn't understand why he was telling me that, especially if it had any validity to it. I knew that if an inmate ever got lucky enough to get chummy with a female staff member, they both needed to be scrupulous about it because they could've ended up in lots of trouble. I figured that he was either deluding himself, or that he viewed me as a potential threat and had only told me that to keep me from pursuing her. What he actually did was direct my attention towards her even more.

I began to notice that they did have some type of connection because they were always talking and laughing together. I can't lie, I was becoming a bit jealous deep down because he was getting all of her attention, and she hadn't begun noticing me yet. I was just "Born, the new guy". He had been working there for a while. He also lived in the same dorm as me. I think that he liked my style because he would sometimes approach me and make small talk with me. I even heard him repeat my slang once or twice. Most times, he would mention that female's name for some reason. It almost felt like he was gloating and rubbing it in my face. One day, I decided to test him. He mentioned that he wanted to have sex with her, so I replied, "Word? I want to have sex with her too". His eyes told me that he didn't like my remark but he tried to play it cool. He responded, "I ain't mad at you. Do you".

About one week later, rumors began circulating about him and her being under investigation and her taking a polygraph test. On the very same night that I heard that rumor, he came to me and voluntarily told me that exact same story. Thats when I learned that she had passed the polygraph test. He started going from person to person and collecting stamped envelopes because he believed that he was about to be placed in Lock Up, due to his involvement with her. That next day, I had to work and I was there when her shift began. When she came to work, she had an embarrassed look on her face and she couldn't look anyone directly into their eyes. Everyone had heard the skinny by then. A few days later, the guy was taken to Lock Up as he'd predicted.

As the days passed, she was starting to notice me. We might've shared a few words sporadically. Never about anything personal though. After almost two weeks, the guy was released from Lock Up and assigned to a different dorm. He came into the cafeteria to eat lunch one day while she was working. I observed how she reacted when she spotted him, and how they interacted with one another. She seemed happy to see him and they were mouthing words to each other from a distance, reading each other's lips. Again, I became slightly jealous. This went on everytime that he came into the mess hall to eat with his dorm. It got to the point where I would turn and look the other way because I didn't like the sight of it all. In my dorm, rumors were starting to circulate about why they had went under investigation. It turned out that the guy had been telling multiple inmates that he had sex with her. I overheard two guys say that he had told them that personally.

I began working with her more, and getting more acquainted. She was married with four children, plus she was a couple of years older than I was. I would never mention the other guy. He didn't seem like much of a factor anymore. She no longer seemed to be giving him much attention when he came through. Our friendly conversations led to flirting and staring into each other's eyes oftentimes. I could tell that she was starting to feel for me in the same way that I was feeling for her. Then, one day, I asked her how she thought I felt about her. She replied, "You think I'm cool". I asked, "Is that it?". Then she asked, "What are you trying to give off?". I explained that it was complicated because she was married and I was incarcerated. Then I admitted that, if I was free, I would pursue her; married or not. She said that, if I was home, the feelings would be mutual. I guess thats the point when I realized that I had a shot.

The flirting, conversations and stares continued and, before I knew it, I was working double shifts and even going in on my days off. The conversations became more and more personal. I decided to be 100% honest with her about everything. Over the years, I've come to learn that the longest lasting friendships, relationships, business endeavors and etc., are the ones that are built upon truth. I told her that I had been on a guilt trip for years because I had lost an ex-girlfriend due to me being irresponsible, philandering with other women, and putting my hands on her. She actually minimized it like it wasn't that serious. Then she explained that she and her husband had a few physical altercations of their own throughout their marriage.

This woman and I had some things in common. We were both somewhat hubristic and outspoken. We were both analytical about things. She was philharmonic like me, and we had a similar taste in music. We were both big fans of Jay-Z and Ghostface Killah. We were also both sarcastic. All of my life I've been writing and recording music. She sometimes wrote rap lyrics at her leisure. When she recited four bars from one of her verses for me, it blew me out of the water. She was starting to seem like my soulmate. Sometimes, we would be thinking the same thoughts and we started dreaming about each other. She was the first one to share that she'd been having these dreams. The first time, she said that she had dreamt that I knocked on her door at home one night. When she opened it, I was standing there and I said that I needed a place to crash for the night. Her husband was at work so she invited me inside and made me a pallet on her living room floor. We kissed but before we could have sex, she was awakened by her cat.

After she told me the details about her dream, I made a joke about it. I said, "Damn cat. I hope that you starved him afterwards....beat him or something", and we laughed it off. I started thinking about her all the time and I looked forward to seeing her radiant smile everyday. Her presence in my life gave me the balance that I needed. I believe that the feelings were mutual. It must've been obvious to some of my co-workers that she and I had a connection because, sometimes, they would say things to me like, "Born, I think shorty likes you". I would simply brush them off like I had no clue of what they were talking about.

She was pro-social with everyone but I guess that we gave off a certain aura when we were near each other. It got to the point that whenever we would talk, someone would always seem to be looking into our mouths. Thats when I decided to teach her the ubiquitous language of the Nation of Gods and Earths, known as the Supreme Mathematics. We both spoke basic spanish so whenever people were around, we would mix all three languages (english, spanish and Supreme Mathematics) when we spoke; just to confuse the eavesdroppers who would attempt to read our lips.

I liked her because she was sharp and seemed really artful at being discrete. It was almost scary and I would sometimes be suspicious of her; wondering if our connection was a big game to her, and if I was just another pastime for her while she was at work. One day I walked past her and I mouthed the words "I love you" to her. I'm not sure of whether she read my lips or not but I asked her about it one hour later and she said that she didn't. She then asked what it was that I had said. I replied that I was shy and that I preferred not to repeat it. She badgered me until I finally relented, "Okay, I said I love you". Then she said, "Okay, next time say it where I can hear it". I replied, "You just did". Then she said, "I love you too". That opened the floodgates because I started to tell her that I loved her at every given opportunity. She would say it in return but I started to feel some type of way when I realized that I was always the first to say it.

I decided that I wasn't going to say it again unless she said it first. For the next few days, when it became time for me to return to my dorm; I would simply say "Peace" or "I'll see you tomorrow". One day, I had to work in the S.M.U. kitchen where we prepared the meals for the inmates who were in Lock Up. She worked that day but she worked in the cafeteria where the general population was fed. There was a different female supervising us. That afternoon when her shift was over, she stopped by the S.M.U. kitchen on her way out of the prison to go home. This was atypical of her and I knew that I was her real reason for stopping by. I was cleaning up my work station and preparing to return to my dorm when she walked in. She greeted everyone and pretended to be inspecting our work. Then, when no one was looking, she mouthed the words "I love you" to me. I returned her words, then she asked, "Are you happy now that you know you've got me open?". I replied, "You have me open too".

It was like we had some type of telepathy going on, almost metaphysical; the way that she picked up on how and why I had stopped saying "I love you" everyday. I believed that we had something real, even though we'd never made any verbal commitment. One day I said to her, "I want to ask you something but I'm apprehensive about asking because I don't like rejection". She replied, "I don't like rejection either, but ask anyway". I hesitated until I finally found the courage to ask, "Can I kiss you?". She looked at me and said, "No". I shrugged and said, "Oh well", feeling like I had played myself with my little romantic overture. Then, she said, "But that wasn't rejection, it was principle". I asked, "Why? Because you're married?". She answered, "No, because of where we are. But I'm glad that you asked". It was clear that we were becoming more than friends so I asked her what I was to her. She said that she didn't want to put a label on what we had so I left it at that.

One day, she asked me and another guy to come with her to the walk-in freezer to retrieve a few bags of milk. She held the door open for us while we carried the milk out. I was the last man out. As I was about to pass by her, I noticed that she was looking the other way and that the other guy wasn't paying us any attention. Thats when I stole a kiss on her cheek. I tried to kiss the corner of her lips but I missed. I walked away briskly with a smirk on my face. I didn't want to look back to see how she was looking at me. When I finally did, she had a scowl on her face; staring at me like I had violated in a major way. I was thinking, "Born, either you're about to get a charge or she's gonna slap the shit out of you". When I walked past her a few minutes later, I tried to look serious like I was upset. I was actually feeling edgy because I thought that someone had stolen the book that I had brought to work that day. It was Torchlight for America by the honorable minister Louis Farrakhan.

I asked her, "Have you seen the book that I was reading earlier?". She replied, "No", without mentioning the kiss. Thats when I figured that I was off the hook. A little while later, she beckoned me to her office, retrieved my book from her desk drawer and told me not to ever kiss her like that again. When I agreed, she said, "Man, I want to punch you in your face". "Why?", I asked. Then she replied, "I'm kidding, but don't do that again". Before long, she was walking past me and whispering flirts like "Hey boo thang, give me a kiss". She would blow me kisses sometimes and, whenever the opportunity presented itself, I would kiss her on her cheek or on her neck. I could never kiss her lips because she always wore pink or red lip gloss. We tried to be as discrete as possible but the attraction kept growing stronger. Me, being the vulnerable one locked away in prison, I was probably more susceptive than she was. We would walk past each other and deliberately brush up against each other or touch hands in passing.

I decided to ask her where she wanted to go with it because there was no denying our feelings for each other. She said that she had been considering asking me the same question. I reminded her that she had once said that she didn't want to put a label on what we had. She retracted those words so I said that I wanted a relationship with her, and she accepted. I asked if she was in love with her husband and she replied, "No, but I used to be". She said that their marriage was eventually going to end and that she was only sticking around for the children's sake. It never sat well with me that she was going home to him every night. I never asked about what they did together. I tried to dispel those types of thoughts as much as possible. I understood that my circumstances weren't normal and that her situation was convoluted so I was going to have to do some radical compromising.

Another thing that I didn't like was the fact that she partied on the weekends, smoked weed and drunk alcohol occasionally. My main issue with that came when I would hear my co-workers saying how she sometimes mentioned her affinity for partying. Behind her back, they called her promiscuous. I didn't want her to have that type of stigma written on her. I tried to ward off those types of thoughts as well, and just appreciate the pieces of her that I was allowed to have. Plus, the fact that she educed the best in me. Pretty soon, there were more haters, more rumors and more speculations. The supervisors began to hear things about us from their personal informants. Most of the other female supervisors envied her because she got all of the attention from the guys, effortlessly. She exuded so much charm, she had a warm personality, and she would let everyone cook whatever they wanted whenever she was the only supervisor on duty.

The other women didn't like her because she always spoke her mind, having no qualms about who might've gotten offended. Plus, she never let them break her or see her sweat. I adored that about her and she reminded me of myself in that sense. Most of my co-workers didn't like me either. I'd been accused of being smug, grandiloquent, snooty and snobbish. People just didn't know how to take me, and most of them were prejudging me or reading me wrong. I'm the reticent type, naturally, and I rarely speak to strangers. I don't go around looking for friends, especially not in an environment like prison. Prison is filled with undercover snitches, homos, sneak thieves and etc. I'm diametrically opposed to all of the above. Everyone is suspect to me so, when a stranger approaches me, almost off of reflex I sneer at them. Thats because I'm wondering what their ulterior motives are, and to let them know that I'm not gullible by far.

Most of my co-workers had crushes on the woman that I was involved with. When they began to notice our chemistry, they started to loathe me even more. The head supervisor despised her. She was always nit-picking at her, giving her a hard time and trying to provoke her to resign. When her snitches told her that she and I had something going on, I became Public Enemy #1 in that kitchen. Two of the female supervisors, who were friends with my girl, warned me to move meticulously because they were told to fire me at the first given opportunity. Another supervisor had it out for me. She was afraid of the head supervisor and was hell bent on impressing her for brownie points. She would basically bully me when she worked, trying to provoke me to quit. She would assign me to the worst tasks. Things got so bad that my name was written in the log book. They said that I wasn't allowed to work on my days off. We couldn't even speak to each other at work. We had to ignore each other or covertly say a few words in passing.

I didn't own a cellphone but a partner of mine would let me hold his for two or three nights a week. He was under scrutiny and the contraband officers were always searching his cell. I gave her the number to that cellphone but she never called it. She would never give me her telephone number and I assume that was because she lived with her husband. It actually took me months to get her to disclose her Facebook name to me. I began inboxing her, using the language called Supreme Mathematics. Then, one day, she replied and said that we couldn't inbox each other anymore because she was worried that her superiors could've found out. I told her that her messages wouldn't be accessible to anyone unless they knew her password. Then I added that since we weren't Facebook friends, they had no way of knowing that we were inboxing each other. Still, she was opposed to it. She agreed to create a new profile under an alias name but she never did it.

It felt quirky to me that she wasn't trying to find ways to keep our lines of communication open, since we were both basically banned from each other on the job. Deep down, I began to question her love for me. I did consider the facts that her job, her livelihood, and her marriage were all at stake; but I still felt like she could've done more to show me that the feelings were still reciprocal. I would also get jealous when it seemed like she was giving other guys on the job more attention than me. She always claimed that she was doing that intentionally to counter the rumors about us.

One day, the inevitable happened. As I did everyday, I walked over to the Therapeutic Diet serving line and fixed me a tray of fruits to eat. By the policy, I wasn't supposed to do that but most of the supervisors never minded when I did because they knew that I was a vegetarian. My girl especially didn't mind. I slipped up this day because our arch nemesis, the head supervisor, was working that afternoon. When she spotted me with a tray of peaches, she made a big deal out of it and fired me on the spot. My girl was also there and she was standing nearby when I got fired. When it happened, it was like the music just stopped. I looked at her and she looked hurt, plus disappointed in me.

Before I returned to my dorm, I was able to hold a brief conversation with her; despite the fact that she was upset with me and didn't really want to talk. I apologized and then I reasoned with her that everything happened for the best because they were going to put a stop to us eventually. I said that if it would've happened any other way, she might've been unemployed, her husband could've found out, and I would've been in Lock Up for inmate/staff relations. At least I could still see her for a few minutes each day when I came into the mess hall to eat with my dorm. She remained upset because the backlash fell on her when the head supervisor accused her of allowing me to get the tray of fruits. Still, she agreed to resume communicating with me via Facebook.

The next few days required some adjusting because I had became attached to her, and now I could hardly even see her. All that I could do was basically say hi and bye everyday. That same week, I received an order to report to my caseworker and she informed me that I would be getting transferred to another prison soon. When I explained this to her, she seemed indifferent about it. Maybe it was because other people were around. On that Friday, I learned that I was getting transferred on that following Monday. I told her the news the next morning and she still seemed nonchalant about the whole situation.

When Monday came around, I had an order to report to the holding cell at 3:15 a.m., which was around the same time that she would've been opening up the cafeteria for the inmate workers to report to work. I had held on to my work boots after I got fired so that I could have an excuse to go to the mess hall one day when she was the only supervisor working. I had opted to go under the guise of me needing to return my boots. When I realized that I was getting transferred, Monday morning became that opportune moment.

On my way to the holding cell that morning, I made a detour. I slipped into the mess hall with my boots in hand, after I spotted her through the window. There weren't any inmate workers in the cafeteria yet but there was a group of workers on their way, not very far behind me. She looked surprised to see me. We said our "goodbyes" and "I love yous" as the workers began filtering in. I began to walk towards the exit door but I decided to turn around, and I walked back to her. She automatically began shaking her head "no" like she believed that I was about to try something that might've jeopardized her job. I just said, "Give me a hug, there's no one behind me". I knew that we had about 15 seconds before someone would bend the corner and come to the spot where we were standing. We hugged and I kissed her cheek as I pulled away. Then, we both said "I love you" again and I exited the cafeteria.

I reported to the holding cell with her on my mind, and her scent on my uniform. About fifteen other inmates and I boarded the bus with handcuffs on our wrists and shackles on our ankles. Normally, on transportation runs, I would look out of the window for the entire ride; trying not to even blink and miss a millisecond of what was going on in society. This particular morning, I laid down in the backseat and stared at the overhead surface of the bus for the majority of the ride. I was thinking about her and reflecting back on the times that we had spent together, wondering if we were going to keep in touch or if I would ever see her again.

When I arrived at my next facility, I bought a cellphone on my second day there. Then, I inboxed her my new number on Facebook. She never called, texted or inboxed me back. During the next week, I sent her two lengthy messages. She never responded but I noticed that she had seen them already. I checked out her profile picture and noticed that some guy had commented on it about four days prior to that day. He commented, "Damn ma, those lips". She commented back, "I can say the same thing about yours". I became upset. When that happens, I can be very scurrilous and have a critical tongue. My mother calls it a pink tornado. I had a talent for calling out a person's biggest insecurities to hurt them. What usually happened was that I said things and ended up hurting myself more than the person who I intended to hurt. I inboxed her and said some egregious things. In hindsight, it was juvenile. But, in the heat of the moment, it felt warranted. On the next day, I finally got a response.

She gave an excuse for not giving a timely response, but she mainly wanted to fire back at me. She scoffed at me by ending her message with the words, "Peace God...lmao". I refrained from sending her any messages for about two months. Within that course of time, I had my eyes on another woman who was a c.o. at my new prison. Plus, since I owned a cellphone, I had other females to call when I needed company. They kept me occupied even though I would often burden them with conversations about her. When I finally did inbox her again, I apologized, brought her up to speed with what was going on in my life, and I told her that I still loved her. She responded with these words only: "Many people love the idea of you but lack the maturity to handle the reality of you". It wasn't the reply that I wanted but I was actually happy to see that she had given me a timely response. Still, I realized that I was at an impasse with her.

I told her that she was right and I admitted to being childish because I wanted to move forward if possible. I didn't see the logic in bickering back and forth. She never replied so I fell back once again. Shortly afterwards, I caught a charge for possession of gang paraphernalia. A contraband officer searched my living area and discovered the book How to Hustle and Win by Dr. Supreme Understanding in my locker. He said that the book was gang related and had me transferred on the following day. I decided to take a risk by smuggling my phone into my next prison, hidden inside of a food item. It worked.

This particular prison was different from every other prison that I had been in. No one had cellphones and the dorms were open bay. "Open bay" means that there are no individual cells. To get a visual; think about the inside of the prison dorm on the movie Life, or the military barracks in the movie Forrest Gump. Or, just imagine a capacious room with 56 beds in it, each bed being only two feet apart from the next. My bed area didn't have an electrical outlet near it so I needed to befriend someone who had one. That way I could keep my phone charged. On my second day, by happenstance, I bumped into a guy who I used to let hold my phone every night at my previous prison. He had gotten into some trouble and was transferred there two weeks before I was. I always felt like he was kind of flighty, but he had an electrical outlet beside his bed and I didn't know anyone else.

I told him to move carefully with my phone and not to let anyone see him with it. He acquiesced but in my heart I believed that he would be ostentatious with it. He was acting over-zealous about me being the only person there with a phone. On my third night, I was lying in my bed; under the covers, with my coat covering my head and the upper part of my body. It was approximately 11:30 p.m. I still didn't know anyone in my pod. The guy who charged my phone for me lived in a different pod. I was underneath my coat, talking on my phone. I always laid perfectly stiff so that the other inmates would think that I was asleep. I would speak softly into the phone and, because of all of the background noise from other inmates talking, no one could hear me. Little did I know, the guy who was charging my phone up for me had been showing my phone off to his roommate who was a gangmember.

Other members of that gang lived in my pod. They were on to me but I didn't know it. All of a sudden, I felt someone grab me. I panicked at first, assuming that it was an officer. This burly dark-skinned guy snatched me out of my bed and restrained me in a bearhug position from behind. I was sort of dazed because he had just snatched me out of my relaxation where I had been lying on my stomach. I realized that it wasn't an officer when I saw about ten gangmembers surrounding my bed, some clutching knives. I was still clutching my phone in my fist but the charger was beneath my pillow. Two of the gangmembers punched me in my face a couple of times, causing me to drop the phone. They released me after one of them picked the phone up.

While they were jumping me, one kid was breaking into my locker and he stole my Walkman. Then, I watched all of them walk into a corner with my phone. They were celebrating like they had just won the Powerball. Since I was outnumbered, I had to swallow that one that night. I don't believe in going to the authorities so I went to my bed area and put my boots on. I needed to be better prepared in case they tried to attack me again. My top lip was swelling, I could taste the blood in my mouth, and I was heated but there was nothing that I could do. After a while, I didn't feel comfortable with sitting down anymore so I began pacing around my bed area. Then, five of the guys who had robbed me called me over to their huddle.

I walked over with my head held high and my chest poked out. They asked why I had put my boots on and if I was thinking about retaliating. They said that they were thinking about stabbing me up. I replied with something to the effect of, "Of course I don't like what you did but I can't win against ten niggas with swords. I've gotta charge this one to the game. Y'all did that. I don't think you realize who you did it to, but you did it. I ain't a bitch, and none of y'all could've done that alone. Now, you don't have to worry about me going to the cops. I ain't going to sneak anybody in their sleep. And, I'm not going to protective custody. Just change my number, delete my pictures and all of my contacts".

For the next few days, there was a lot of tension in the air and a lot of grouping-up going on. They were constantly watching me to see who I spoke to, and if I was shopping around for a weapon. I still remained reclusive although a few strangers were coming to me and saying that they had my back if I wanted to retaliate. They said that they were tired of that gang getting away with robbing people. I didn't know who to trust so I always kept the conversations brief. The situation was burning me up so bad that one day I went to one of the gang's leaders and asked for a one-on-one fist fight with one of them. He granted me that and let me choose which one I wanted to fight. I chose the one who had told me that they were thinking about stabbing me up. A few Bloodmembers who I had recently met accompanied me to assure that I didn't get jumped. We fought in the inmate restroom. I didn't thrash him like I wanted to but he and his partners got the message.

The idea to ask for a one on one fight or to stab a few of them in their sleep was heavy on my mind, but I hesitated for the sake of my niece and nephew. They had just gotten approved on my visitation list for the first time in eight years, and my mother had planned to bring them to visit me that weekend. They were excited about visiting me. Initially, I was opposed to it because my lip was all swollen and I didn't want for them to see me like that. Especially when seeing me for the first time in eight years.

My mother convinced me that they weren't concerned about that and she emphasized that they really wanted to see me. I decided to control my anger because I didn't want to avert the visit by getting into trouble. When I walked into the visitation room that Saturday morning, my niece and nephew didn't recognize me. I don't know if it was because of my lip or because they hadn't seen me in eight years. The first thirty minutes of the visit seemed awkward for them but, before long, we were all laughing and joking together. It was a great visit. A day or two later is when I got into the fight.

I never recovered my phone because one of the guys got caught with it four days after they had robbed me. That following week was weird because, one by one, all of the guys involved in my robbery got into some type of trouble and were removed from our dorm. One guy caught an extortion charge on another inmate. Two of them got caught jumping someone. And, one of them got caught with some K-2. The others got packed up for reasons that are unknown to me. A few of them began sending me threats from Lock Up, accusing me of snitching and setting them up. We all knew that it was simply karma working. You do dirt, and you get mud. I had my sister to inbox my kitchen supervisor friend, and inform her about the incident. She replied that she was happy that I was okay. That was the last thing that I heard from her up until the date of this writing.

The above incident taught me a valuable lesson that I believe was imperative for me to learn before being reposited into society. For many years of my life, I was in the armed robbery game. Until it actually happened to me, I never realized how repulsive and dastardly it is to take something from an innocent and defenseless person. I can now say, unequivocally, that I will never even consider doing something like that again. That incident also made me more circumspect.

19

A Mother's Love

When I was a younger man, one of the pivotal people in my life explained to me that the black woman, as a part of her intrinsic nature, has the power of cultivation. That translates to her having the power to make people relax, loosen up and open up to her. She's just wired that way. Thats what enables her to stop babies from crying, simply by holding them in her arms and whispering soft words to them. However, those powers can be employed in both positive and negative ways; depending on the mentality of the woman.

One example of how this power can be used negatively is in the well-known Biblical tale of Samson the Nazarite and Delilah the Philistine. Delilah was a woman who was hired by the lords of the Philistines to use her cultivation powers to make Samson divulge to her the source of his strength. Without that knowledge, the Philistines could not overpower Samson. Delilah's orders were to entice him with dulcet words, massages and sex. They promised her 1,100 pieces of silver if she was successful.

Samson seemingly knew from the inception that Delilah's intentions were impure. Three times, she asked him to entrust his secret to her and he mocked her each time. He told her lies as a subterfuge to avoid being captured. She persisted to pester him daily until he finally relented and did what the Bible calls "tell her all his heart". With her cultivation powers, she coaxed him into imparting his secret to her. That mistake turned out to be the start of his ending. Shortly afterwards, he was over-powered and captured.

All women don't use their cultivation powers to emasculate men, although I've had my fair share of women who have tried. However, I am in no way trying to make the black woman out to be the Eve to my Adam. In prison, especially after years and years of incarceration, a man can become vulnerable to women. This is mainly due to the dearth of female companionship. I went through that lonely stage quite a few times. Whenever I did, I found it hard to focus on anything productive like writing my books or litigating my arguments for my appeal. I believed that was because I didn't have homeostasis in my life - an inner balance that I felt like I could only get from the black woman. At times, being without a female felt like I had been chopped in half.

One night, I was feeling so lonely and despondent that I called a friend of mine and asked him to introduce me to a female who I could talk to. That friend was Dino. He gave me the name and cellphone number that belonged to a young lady named Joy, one of his cd customers. It almost felt like he was setting me up for failure because he told me to call her, but to lie to her if she asked who gave me her number. As I stated in a previous chapter, the best relationships are the ones that are built upon truth. With a sentiment akin to that one in mind, I reluctantly sent Joy a text message. As expected, she replied and her first question was how I got her cellphone number. I lied, using the story that Dino told me to use. I told her that I had met her a while back at a convenience store. That was a debacle waiting to happen because I had been incarcerated for about four years by that point. She replied with certitude that she had never given me her number.

Instead of perpetuating that same lie, I confessed the truth to her. I admitted that a friend of mine had given me her number and that I had promised not to tell her who he was. I explained that I was immured and that I was just looking for a friend, as pathetic as it sounds. Then, I said that I would understand it if she chose to preclude any further communication with me, because I had planned to keep my promise to Dino. It took her about thirty minutes to respond. When she did, she said that she suspected that I was her ex-boyfriend playing a trick on her. I told her that I was telling the truth about who I was and she believed me. Then she empathized with me and gave me permission to call her. At the time, she was also in a vulnerable stage. She was still in love with her ex-boyfriend who was disacknowledging her and expecting a baby with a white woman.

Joy was very attractive in appearance, and in personality. She was just so hung up over her ex-boyfriend that she didn't seem interested in having anything with me, other than a platonic friendship. She also understood that I still had approximately ten years remaining on my sentence, so I have to factor that in as well. Joy and I began conversing daily and nightly over the phone. She consulted me whenever she needed sage advice, even when it pertained to her and her ex-boyfriend. At that time, I was interested in Joy but I would still proffer my unbiased opinions and advice.

Early in our friendship, I learned that Joy and I had a common thread. Ever since she was a young girl, she had a proclivity towards being a writer. She was attending college and majoring in mass communications writing. During that time, I was in the process of self-publishing my first novel, Moving Target. In my opinion, Joy was a better writer than I was. She was more of a natural, and ideas came to her melifluously. Creating good stories from my imagination was more like an arduous task for me, initially an experiment to see if I could do it.

When I published Moving Target, I had my mother to send Joy a copy of the galley proof. I wanted to inspire her to continue writing and to show her that getting a book published was very possible. Even more so for her since she was out in society with access to a lot more resources than I had access to. She seemingly began to take her writing more earnestly after that. She encouraged me to write another book and thats when I began writing my sophomore novel, entitle Promise: A Bloody Love Story. Promise is the name of the main character in that book. I used that name because I had decided long ago that I would name my first daughter Promise. I considered the fact that I had a decade left in prison and decided to use the name for my main character instead.

Joy and I would spend hours reading our chapters to each other and exchanging ideas. She was working on four different books at once, which I always protested against. I suggested that she focused her attention on one book, completed it and then proceeded to the next one. She wasn't as focused as I was because she was distracted by the vices of the outside world - mainly partying, smoking and drinking. She was also having trouble recuperating from her break-up with her ex-boyfriend.

She was extremely emotional and sometimes she would cry to me. It actually began to feel like I was the one with the cultivation powers because my voice always seemed to cause her to loosen up and begin crying. It was obvious that she had a lot going on beneath the surface, and I always believed that there were some important things that she wasn't telling me about her life.

I had developed love for Joy and I made it my duty to be her crying shoulder whenever she needed me. Some nights we would fall asleep on the phone together, and I would wake up to her snoring lightly on the other end. Then I would press a button on the phone to awake her. At one time, Joy didn't own a cellphone so she would call me from her mother's cellphone. When Joy finally bought a cellphone of her own, I still kept her mother's number saved in my contacts. She and her ex-boyfriend were still seeing each other, although I didn't know the intricate details about their dealings. All I knew was that, if I called and she didn't answer, she was probably with him. On one particular afternoon, Joy called me; crying hysterically because he had just punched her in her face for accosting his white girlfriend. Oddly, Joy still wanted to be with him.

Almost two weeks later, I called Joy's cellphone and her ex-boyfriend answered it. He must've seen my name on the screen of her phone. He didn't say anything to me. Instead, he asked her who I was. He was raising his voice and I heard her begin to explain that I was only a friend, and that I was incarcerated. Suddenly, he hung up the phone. It was around midnight. I began to worry that he was going to attack her again, and I got upset because being in prison hampered me from doing anything to defend her. Thats when I decided to send her mother a text message. The message read: "This is Joy's friend, Born. I think that Joy may be in trouble". In a matter of seconds, she texted me back, "Call me".

I called immediately and explained why I believed that Joy was in danger. I told her that Joy's ex-boyfriend had punched her in her face two weeks prior to that night. The problem was that Joy wasn't answering her phone and neither one of us knew her whereabouts. Her mother told me that she was about to get dressed, and drive around the town in attempt to find her. I told her to call me whenever she found her and that I would be up all night, awaiting her call. She found Joy in a couple of hours and her ex-boyfriend had indeed tried to hurt her.

I believe that, as of that night, her mother took a liking to me. I don't think that she was very fond of most of the people who Joy circulated with. Based on what Joy would tell me, they were mostly weedheads, alcoholics and people who didn't have much going for themselves. I always felt that they were bad company for her, and I encouraged that she sought out better friends - people who were smarter than her, and people who didn't have the same problems that she had. Whenever I would call her mother's house, her mother would always be congenial with me. I could've called early in the morning or late at night, and she would always seem happy to know that I was interested in her daughter. If Joy would've been asleep, she would've tried to awake her.

I later began to learn some things about Joy's mother. She had been living with breast cancer ever since Joy was a young girl. She was a school teacher, and she was also adept in writing. She had actually begun writing a children's book about her cancer situation. After learning all of this, I realized why she was always affable towards me. She realized that I was a true friend to Joy, and that I would always push her to do the right things if anything ever happened to her. She saw that I wasn't just a talker when it came down to my book publishing business. She wanted to see Joy live out her dream of becoming a published author, and she knew that she would be in good hands if she worked with me. I truly believe that she wanted to see Joy and I in a relationship, despite the predicament that I was in.

This woman became like a second mother to me. I would call their home and wind up speaking with her for a while, whenever Joy wasn't home. She eventually began writing me letters. In those letters, she always explained that she was happy that her daughter had met me. She said that Joy had changed for the better after meeting me. She would send me information that she printed from the internet about how I could get free legal counsel to assist me with my appeal. She also told me that she wanted me to help her to publish her book when she finished writing it. Of course, I agreed to help her.

As we became closer, her cancer battle began to concern me. I took the initiative to study about the causes of breast cancer, and what she could eat or do to combat against it. There were two books that I found to be of the most service. They were How to Eat to Live by the honorable Elijah Muhammad, and The Hood Health Handbook by Dr. Supreme Understanding. I jotted down notes from those books. Then, I wrote her a letter to enlighten her about natural healing and eating healthy foods. She corresponded back to me, thanked me for my help, and agreed to begin practicing healthy dieting.

A few months later is when I got jumped and robbed for my cellphone. I was unable to buy another cellphone for nine months, because there were no phones available to buy. I called Joy once or twice on 3-way during that period, but I didn't speak to her mother. I would only inquire about her condition and tell Joy to let her know that I was still praying for her convalescence. I eventually got transferred to a different facility and was able to call Joy more frequently. On the first time that I reached Joy, she began to cry upon the recognition of my voice. Immediately, I assumed that her mother had just transcended.

The phone call was only for about four minutes and I exhausted the first two minutes by trying to placate her. I continued to ask her what was wrong but her words couldn't come out because of her wailing and convulsive gasping. When she finally pulled herself together, she explained that her mother was doing fine. She said that she was just emotionally spent because she had recently lost her job and was malcontent with her life in general. I guess that she had also been missing me since I hadn't been available for her to cry to in a while. Even if that was the case, I still felt like she was acting overly dramatic.

Approximately two weeks passed before I called Joy again. When she answered, I greeted her, "Hey beautiful". She recognized my voice immediately. Then, in a dismal voice, she said, "Born, guess what". Before I could guess, she informed me that her mother had passed away two days prior to that day. I consoled her and gave her my condolences. Thats when she assured me that she would be fine. She said that she wanted me to call more frequently because her mother had finished writing her book before she passed. She needed for me to help her publish it. Without second-guessing, I agreed to help her.

After giving it some thought, I began to consider that when I had called Joy that first time; maybe her mother's death had something to do with her reason for crying, even though she hadn't died yet. As I mentioned in a previous chapter, I had a similar experience when my best friend Travis died. This may sound quirky to some readers but I, personally, don't place limitations on the mind or it's functions.

20

CHILD'S PLAY

L ets imagine for a second that we were on the television
game show, Family Feud. And, I was your host, comedi-
an/actor Steve Harvey. I would begin round one by asking the
simple question, "In one single word, tell me something that
a child does?". I'm sure that the number one answer would be
"play". One thing that I've always had an issue with throughout my years of incarceration was the fact that so many of
our black men in prison waste time by playing. Grown men
with major responsibilities, all day long saying, "Lets play
cards, chess, dominoes, handball, or basketball". If not that,
its "Who saw the game on tv last night?" or "Who's playing
on tv tonight?". One thing that always jumped out at me was
the fact that the words "play" and "game" both denote child-

ishness.

The majority of the inmates who I know had sired children prior to their incarceration. Some of them have been removed from their children's lives for five, ten, fifteen, twenty years or more. In those cases, how much time do any of them have to squander by playing? Just imagine if their children could turn into flies, fly into the prisons, post up on the walls and monitor their fathers' daily activities. Their little buggy eyes would be flooded with tears after seeing how their fathers are playing and being prodigal with their time, instead of doing everything within their powers to return home to them and their mothers.

All day long, I would see and hear these grown men, filled with exuberance and shouting at the top of their lungs about someone throwing out the wrong playing card, someone moving their chess piece out of turn, or someone getting fouled on the basketball court. Oftentimes, fights would stem from these petty disagreements and people would get hurt or possibly killed. In most cases, there would be gambling involved. The bets were usually minuscule; worth no more than a $2.00 food item. A lot of guys wouldn't have any money at all so they would place bets for push-ups on demand. That means that the loser would have to drop and do any given amount of push-ups at the behest of the winner, whenever or wherever he demanded it. I've even seen instances where the loser had to shave off his eyebrows or make humiliating animal sounds on demand.

When violence would result from these penny ante bets, most times the parties involved would insist that they were only fighting because of "the principle", not the food or hygiene item. Just like a bunch of fourth graders on their elementary school's playground at recess, there would be peers applying pressure (directly or indirectly) for both parties to go through with the fight. Testosterone becomes involved and, before you know it, two guys are at each other's throats over a pack of no-frills cookies.

Another game thats often played is what I call the "Who knows the most about nothing?" game. Its when inmates waste countless hours on malarkey that serves their own lives no purpose. Typical conversations surround which rappers are the wealthiest, sports stats, which rapper is the most gangster, and who the "baddest" female in the entertainment industry is. These conversations often turn disrespectful and, eventually, violent.

As I'm writing on this particular subject, three things are jumping out at me. The first thing is the 6th degree in the honorable Elijah Muhammad's English C-1 lesson where he wrote: "He likes the devil because the devil gives him nothing". That line was written to describe the mental condition of the so-called American negro. In this degree, I interpreted the word "devil" as meaning more than an evil spirit, an individual caucasian person, or even the caucasoid race in it's entirety. Instead, it represents the system thats being used to program our minds and distract us from realizing the actual genocide thats occurring right before our eyes.

This system is comprised of many components such as foods, drugs, prison, birth control and religion. Just to name a few. And, lets not forget about popular culture - the music and other various sources of entertainment where most of our black youths receive their influence to become gangmembers, drug abusers, alcoholics, criminals, womanizers, homosexuals, and irresponsible parents.

The other two phrases that are jumping out at me are the "Stockholm Syndrome" and the "Patty Hearst Syndrome". Both of these expressions describe the mental condition in which the captive has begun to identify with the captor. I'm sure that most of you readers have seen the movie X, starring

Denzel Washington. This is the film where he portrayed the minister Malcolm X. There's a scene in that movie where he describes the condition of the so-called negro slave. The slave, when referring to the slavemaster, would use the pronoun "we". When concerned about the slavemaster's well-being, he would ask, "Massa, we sick?". That scene always came to mind when I would hear those sports fanatics using those very same personal pronouns in reference to their favorite teams. "Massa, are we playing tonight?". "I hope that we make it to the Super Bowl this year". "Who are we playing?". It always perplexed me, how they would superimpose themselves on teams whose actual members and owners didn't even know that they existed.

When I think about some of our affluent black athletes, I'm reminded of another degree that the honorable Elijah Muhammad included in the 120 lessons, which he wrote in 1934. That degree is the 15th degree in the Lost and Found Lesson #2. It asks, "Who are the 10%?". To be succinct, the 10% represents the elite and rich ruling class of the world who rule by telling lies. The answer to the above question begins with, "They are the rich slavemakers of the poor....". I've always looked at the term "rich slavemakers" as being ambiguous. It could be interpreted to mean that the people who make slaves out of the poor are rich. Or, it could mean that they are making rich slaves.

Most black athletes and entertainers are slaves and don't even realize it. They are blinded by their own opulence. They, themselves, are tools being used to keep the minds of the masses distracted. They are also expendable. If any of them should ever decide to go against the tide and stand up against the system thats oppressing the black nation, they will be silenced. That would be political suicide for them. As easily as their riches were given, they can also be stripped away.

The sad reality of the black inmates who suffer from the two syndromes that I mentioned earlier is that they have no will or ambition to become great themselves. They are so much consumed in the lives of their idols that, somewhere along the line, they forget to create legacies of their own. They could tell you everything there is to know about their favorite football player, but couldn't tell you what their daughter's favorite color is. They could tell you Jay-Z's net worth, but couldn't give you the directions to the prison's Law Library. Some people say that every inmate's case has some type of loophole in it that could get them out of prison early. Sometimes it could be right before their eyes, and other times it could be like finding a needle in a haystack. I'm sure that their children would prefer that their fathers were rummaging through that haystack instead of trying to be the next Bobby Fisher of the penitentiary.

I read once in a book about drug addiction where an author wrote, "If you spend more money on drugs and alcohol than you do on food, then your priorities are misdirected". I say that if you spend more time playing games in prison than you do in working on your craft, planning for your future, communicating with your children, and fighting for your freedom; then your priorities being misdirected is a huge understatement.

Another thing that I couldn't learn to appreciate was seeing grown men horseplaying all of the time. I could never make any logic out of why they did that. I always saw it as inappropriate for men to be wrestling and grabbing on each other, especially in prison. I'll admit that I can be a bit extreme at times but whenever I would see two or more inmates horseplaying, I would interpret it as homosexual behavior, and that would preclude any future dealings with those individuals.

The prisons would sometimes allow the inmates to have softball tournaments or basketball games where one dorm would select team members to play against team members from a different dorm. Another ploy by the devil. The inmates would have so much zeal about playing that they would go as far as to disrespect team members from the opposing dorm. They would also express that they were proud members of the dorm in which they lived. In those instances, I would always remember the Willie Lynch speech. Willie Lynch, a slave owner from the West Indies, taught the slave owners in Jamestown, Virginia his method of controlling slaves by dividing them according to their many disparities. Before long, slaves were arguing that their master was better than the next slave's master. Or, that their plantation was better than the next slave plantation.

There's another thing that I've always disagreed with, pertaining to the national and college sports fanaticism among inmates. It seemed to build a bridge between the inmates and the officers. When officers and inmates were fans of the same team, they would refer to each other as "we", as if they were members of the team. I would notice how the officers would use those discussions to manipulate the inmates, convincing them that they had a common thread. In turn, the inmates would become comfortable enough to speak freely around them while the officers were only working as spies out to gather intelligence about who was doing what.

Far too often, the inmates forget that the officers are the oppressors and the inmates are the oppressed. There should always exist an imaginary line between the two because, at any given time, that same officer who you hobnob with about your favorite team can be slapping handcuffs on your wrists or spraying your face with pepperspray. There are some officers who seem to try to treat the inmates like they would like to be treated themselves. Even those officers are potential oppressors. We must always remember that oppression is a part of their job profile. When referring to black people in prison, I'd prefer not to use the word "inmate" because its no different from other labels that we were branded with by our oppressors like: nigger, negro, colored, slave, prisoner and etc. Know that, in this book, I'm only using the word "inmate" in common parlance.

I entitled this memoir The Fiery Furnace, a title that was inspired by the Biblical story of Shadrach, Meshach and Abed-nego in the book of Daniel. Over the years, I've grown to understand that the Bible is not a book that was written to serve as an actual past history. The Bible was written in advance, before any of the events therein even occurred. Many of the stories in the Bible are allegorical. They are events that have been happening for years, and are still happening today. The stories are useless if we can't see ourselves within them.

The original authors of the Bible were our black ancestors who were wise scientists. Within their writings they foretold what we as a nation would experience over the span of years to come. Those stories were written as reminders to persevere and endure the suffering that would be bestowed upon us by our oppressors. When I juxtaposed the black man's prison experience with the story of the Fiery Furnace, there was a striking resemblance. The same case scenario when I read, open-mindedly, the story of Jonah in the belly of the great fish. Its not by happenstance that prison is often called the "belly of the beast". Then there's Daniel in the lion's den. The prisons are filled with lions and other savages who are constantly preying victim. The bottom line is that each one of those stories have the same motif - that the black man would endure great suffering but would be victorious in the end because of his faith and his righteousness.

I began to realize that I was Jonah. I was Job. I was Daniel, Shadrach, Meshach and Abed-nego. And, the list continues on. While on the topic of the Bible, I want to call your attention to Revelations 12:12 where it reads, "Woe to the inhabitants of the earth and of the sea! For the devil has come down unto you, having great wrath because he knoweth that he hath but a short time". For centuries, our oppressors have been doing everything within their ability to suppress the true knowledge of God, the devil and the world around us. The reason for this is because of their fear of being destroyed once we become awakened. We can't forget that the crimes that we get imprisoned for were once legal for the white race to commit against us. They legally kidnapped us, robbed us; and in countless ways, murdered us. The earliest form of law enforcement in America was established for the apprehension of runaway slaves. So we need to remember who and what the system was designed for - to keep the black man in limbo.

During slavery in America, for a slave to learn how to read or write was a crime that was punishable by death. To trace this fear and suppression even further back, lets examine the way that Alexander the Great and his people went into Egypt, robbed and destroyed the libraries and mystery schools. Then, out of the blue, emerged some Greek philosopher named Aristotle who purported that he wrote over 1,000 of the books that were actually stolen from Egypt. Then there's Napoleon Bonaparte who shot the nose off of the great statue known as The Sphinx, because he didn't want people to notice the wide nostrils and realize that the Sphinx symbolized the black man. Or, lets fast forward to the time when J. Edgar Hoover organized the Counter Intelligence Program, known as CoIntelPro. Their sole objective was to infiltrate and gather intelligence on every black conscious movement that existed during that time. Then, seek out ways to silence those groups.

In the prisons, its all the same. Every black conscious group is stigmatized as being a security threat group. Their adherents are being harassed, harshfully punished and practically robbed of their literature; all in the name of security. The most-targeted group is the Gods and Earths. The Aryan nation, the Bloods, Crips, Gangster Disciples, and Anarchists don't seem to pose as big a threat. The Nation of Islam and the Rastafarians are also on the enemy's radar. Whenever someone gets caught with any literature that even remotely resembles the Gods and Earths' doctrine, the literature is confiscated, that person is labeled in the system as a security threat and is subject to being frequently harassed and searched. His visitation privileges are temporarily suspended and they are sometimes placed in solitary confinement, or transferred. The prisons have investigators who study this so-called "subversive" literature. All along, they know that we teach the truth and thats what they feel threatened by.

AFTERWORD

All of the stories that I have shared in this book are very true, and I didn't embellish any of them. I deliberately excluded or substituted actual names, left the locations anonymous, and rearranged the chronology of events to prevent the incrimination of the parties involved. I expect that learning about some of my personal experiences will deter some of you readers from making decisions that could possibly land you in prison. Also, I hope that I have inspired some of you to reach out to some of your loved ones who are lost in the system. Now, probably more than ever, they need your love and support.

The Fiery Furnace, by far, is the most-intimate book that I've written thus far. I'm sure that there are many other brothers who are currently serving time, or have already served their time, who have had much worse experiences. These were just some of the most eye-opening experiences that I've had while behind the walls, and I've matured immensely because of them. As I mentioned in the proem for this book, the devil's penal system is designed to destroy us; while capitalizing off of us in the process.

To all of the brothers in prison; whether you're serving a light sentence or a life sentence, stay in the Law Libraries as much as possible. At this point, there is nothing more important than fighting for your freedom. Eventually you will find some type of loophole in your case if you search hard enough. Just know that its not going to be easy. Never become institutionalized and begin losing precious time in watching excessive amounts of television, playing games, holding idle conversations, gangbanging and killing each other. All of those things are counterproductive and they work against your best interest. Return home to your families - your mothers, your wives and your children. When you find yourself putting those things on the backburner, evaluate yourself.

Stay away from the poisonous medications that the prisons prescribe; also the cigarettes, drugs and alcohol. Those vices may temporarily sedate your pain, but they are also conducive to your demise. The prison system is already killing you through the foods that they serve you. Strive to eat the healthiest foods and read as much as you can because knowledge is power. Communicate with your children as much as possible, educate them properly, and fight to prevent the devil from destroying your family unit. Use your time to take inventory of yourself and realize what your character defects are. When you discover them, work hard to eradicate them so that you can exercise your fullest potential when you're released back into society. Thank you for reading this book.

Proper Education Always Causes Elevation

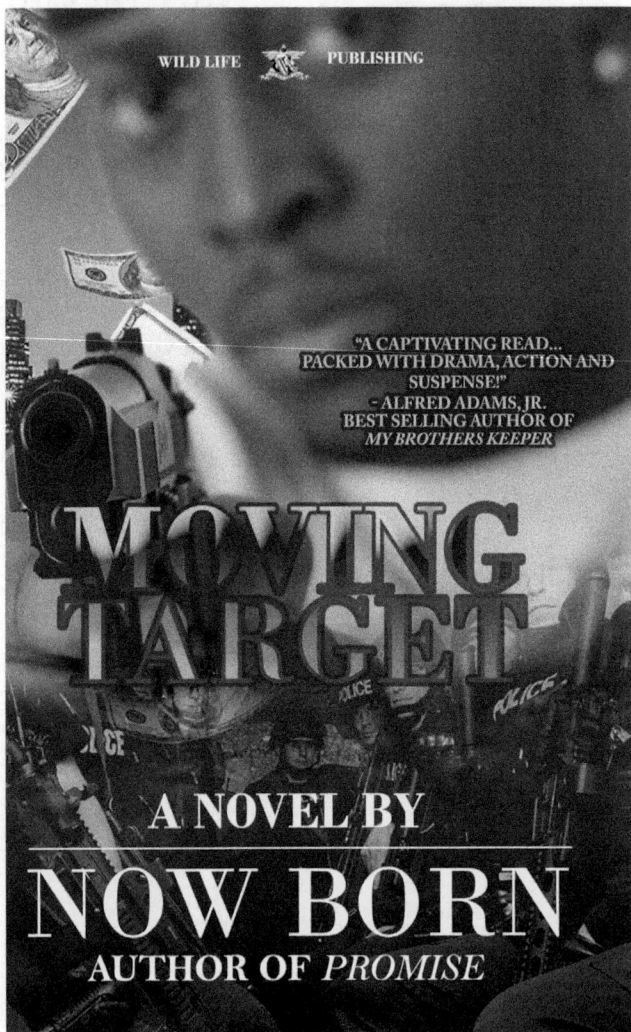

IN BOOK STORES NOW!

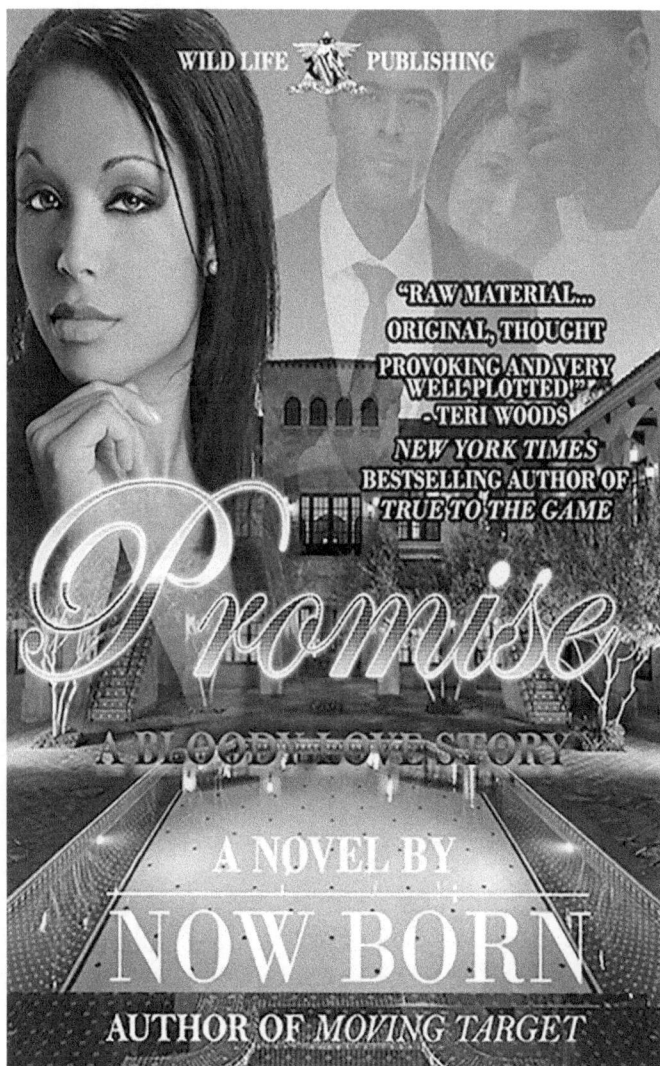

WILD LIFE PUBLISHING

"RAW MATERIAL...
ORIGINAL, THOUGHT
PROVOKING AND VERY
WELL PLOTTED!"
-TERI WOODS
NEW YORK TIMES
BESTSELLING AUTHOR OF
TRUE TO THE GAME

Promise

A BLOODY LOVE STORY

A NOVEL BY
NOW BORN

AUTHOR OF MOVING TARGET